India-China Relations

INDIA-CHINA RELATIONS

1947-1971

Friendship Goes with Power

Part-1

SHRI RAM SHARMA

1999

DISCOVERY PUBLISHING HOUSE

NEW DELHI-110002

First Published-1999

ISBN 81-7141-485-0

© Author

Published by:
DISCOVERY PUBLISHING HOUSE
4831/24, Ansari Road, Prahlad Street,
Darya Ganj, New Delhi-110 002 (*INDIA)*
Phone: 3279245
Fax: 91-11-3253475

Printed at:
Arora Offset Press
Laxmi Nagar, Delhi 110 092.

For

Radha Krishn Sharma

Ardent advocate of cases which, but for his handling, would go by default; phenomenally generous in being helpful but immune to the pangs of ingratitude that is what he often gets in return.

PREFACE

This monograph along with the other two, the one dealing with Indo-US relations and the other tracing Indo-Soviet relations during the years 1947-71, forms part of a major project on Indian foreign policy for which the UGC has been liberal enough to sanction a grant-in-aid. Though the grant period is over, the rest of the project is being pursued with a slight modification required in the preparation of the second part of the survey covering the period from 1971 to the present day. Thus the two parts put together would cover the entire period of contemporary history of Indian foreign policy. This would add significance to the original proposal as well as enhance its suitability as a project complete in itself.

It has generally been believed that India's relations with the three super powers have been so extensive as to include all the major world events in which the two sides, India, on the one hand and each of the three major powers on the other were, under the compulsion of circumstances, forced to get involved, each side invoking high altruistic motives which impelled it to enter into the fray. An objective analysis of the evolving events in a chronological sequence would cover a vast scope of India's total involvement in world affairs. This, in brief, would give us a clear historical perspective of Indian diplomacy in operation during the first fifty years of our life in a sovereign democratic state of our own making.

These essays are mainly addressed to the lay reader who may feel inclined to be familiar with the various aspects of the diplomatic dealings in which the Government at a given time remained preoccupied for reasons which would evoke appreciation from all segments of the society irrespective of any consideration of party

affiliation. After all, the foreign policy of a country, in order to be effective, has to be national both in its objectives as well as the means adopted to achieve them. The problem for the common man has been to be kept informed, in brief and by direct style, of the main landmarks in our international undertakings. This he seeks to do not from the learned treatises which are designed to cater to the tastes of the intellectual elite but from the small occasional publications specifically providing what he should know and what has been the rationale behind each Government move. How far has the author succeeded in his efforts to do what was expected of him would be clear by the extent to which he could manage to sustain the interest of the readership, he had in view to serve, in the basic principles of our foreign policy and how far they were being pursued to achieve one supreme objective namely the preservation, protection and promotion of our national interests.

Shri Ram Sharma

CONTENTS

1

INTRODUCTION

In the real sense, the Sino-Indian relationship both historically and more recently has been empty of real content. In historical times, the export of Mahayan Buddhism from India left no close political ties; it was a state religion in India only for a brief period of Ashok and only spasmodically that of China. Later, even the question of opium did not affect the people to people relations; it was an issue between the qing authorities in China and British East India Company. In pre-independence days both countries were engaged in their own struggle leaving little opportunity for mutual contacts. After the independence of India and liberation of China contacts had been few and far between to mature before being overlaid by strife. There had never been any ideological content in the Sino-Indian dispute as in Sino-Soviet relations, nor the intricacies of East-West relations, nor the ethnic considerations of Indo-Pak ties.[1]

Indian leadership failed to judge the contemporary trends in Chinese policies against the background of Chinese history. The underlying motive for communist China's hostility towards India was derived from the national psychology based on ancient heritage. When they could not co-exist peacefully with the people of long northern region, they preferred isolation which was manifested in the construction of the Great Wall which even till today is regarded as one of the seven wonders of the world. It has also been a symbol of the Chinese people's struggle against the outer world presumed to be hostile. The Middle Kingdom

bounded by the Wall has been an egocentric world of the Chinese people and the core of civilization.[2] Those neighbouring countries which accepted Chinese suzerainty could live with the sufferance of China and those who did not were to be conquered if possible or otherwise ignored.

During the second world war period Lord Wavell, the then governor general of India, one day asked Alfred Caroe, secretary general of the external affairs ministry to prepare a comparison between India and China as future great powers in material resources, manpower and political stability. The general conclusion was that there was not much common in the comparison of the two countries as in his view China was tougher as she had been through the fire both of internal revolutions and external invasions while India was softer having had no such experience. Later the governor general happened to meet A. Dalal, a member of his executive council, and asked him what he thought about the future of the two countries. Dalal also supported the views of Caroe and said that India was too soft and would have to go through the fire before she was able to be a potentially powerful nation to match China.[3]

China's history has run its course in a cyclical order. The cycle would begin when a strong military leader emerged, unified the country and in so doing created a new ruling dynasty. This was always followed by a period of territorial expansion through vigorous military action and then ensued an era of enforced peace. The post-war communist dynasty in China was in the tradition of its predecessors; came to power through strong military action and conquest. The Chinese communists have been dedicated to uniting China and expanding its frontiers to places which they claimed to be theirs. Their main object was to gain control over the mainland without causing conflict with Russia which could be its main challenger in the landward region of the north.

For the last two decades preceding the communist assumption to power, the Chinese have had no peace at home. The civil war from 1927-34 brought death to nearly 10 million people. The Japanese aggression which started almost at the end of the civil war and went up to 1945 took a toll of another million people. Then followed the communist uprising that ended at the end of

September 1949. This trail of bloody events has made the Chinese extremely ruthless and bred a spirit of sanguinary courage. They can become obstinate to the extent of being fanatic.

A little incident involving Kosygin, the Soviet Premier would illustrate this point. When Kosygin decided to meet Chou En-lai in an effort to improve relations between the two countries, he flew to Peking after attending the funeral of Ho Chi-Minh in 1969. Instead of being taken to the city he was kept at Peking airport where he met Chou for two hours. During the course of conversation Kosygin asked Chou En-lai how long he thought it would take to solve their various differences. Chou with a faint snigger replied "a thousand years". Kosygin said he had hoped that they would be able to see some results of their efforts in their life time. 'Well' said Chou on second thought, 'it might take 100 years'. This is how Chinese have learnt the art of negotiations. When they feel to be right in their cause, they refuse to see other man's viewpoint though they may talk of give and take. To them the sole sanction is of power which cannot be challenged by any other party.[4]

The basic motive of Chinese foreign policy has been its quest for world power. Chou En-lai uttered a sort of warning when he said 'China's views must be heard in any settlement of any major international issue'. This he hoped to achieve only when China had first assumed the leadership of Asia. This would be possible only when the U.S. and the Soviet Union were deprived of their influence among the South east Asian countries. At one time China regarded the Soviet Union as dangerous as the US in preventing it from gaining a position of prominence in the region. Soviet Union's alleged attempts to create trouble in Sinkiang were often recollected by the Chinese as those of the American efforts to aid its allies directed against China. For China, the Soviet menace was landward and the American seaward.[5]

As for South Asia which is a much bigger region, both the super powers were set to boost India to become China's rival. It is not surprising that Khrushchev, Kennedy and Nehru were once publicly branded as China's principal enemies. India, for its size, resources and political maturity was considered a potential danger to China's claims for Asian leadership which should go in favour

of China on the strength of three factors, geographical contiguity, long cultural affinity and contribution of Chinese domiciled population in the development of the region.

In relations with India, it all began with Tibet. Tibet has been viewed by Peking as an area into which Chinese population could expand. Historically China was prevented from colonising outer Tibet by lack of easy access and a hostile and independent-minded Tibetan people. Moreover, British empire was there that wanted Tibet to remain a buffer zone protecting India's northern frontiers. During these times, the British acquired some extra territorial rights to make their presence felt there and also to prevent China from exercising its suzerainty beyond certain points. The British withdrawal made it easy for China to colonise Tibet and to extend its line of authority. India, in its turn, felt that it was neither possible nor advisable to retain the rights and privileges which it had inherited from the British but in the new set up some contacts had to be maintained. The government sought to do this by the agreement signed in Peking after protracted negotiations on 29 April 1954.

On the eve of the 1954 agreement, Girija Shankar Bajpai, the then secretary general in the external affairs ministry, suggested to the government that India's commitment to the agreement should rest on two prior conditions; the opening of an Indian consulate at Kashgar in Sinkiang and the recognition of Mc Mahon line as our border limit. The government did not agree to either of the two conditions through the misplaced faith in Chinese good intentions. The opening up of an Indian consulate in Kashgar would have effectively prevented China from constructing the Aksai Chin road through Ladakh with all the subsequent complications which had later arisen.[6]

The Tibetan uprising in March 1959 upset the delicate balance of Sino-Indian relations. As a result of Chinese suppression, thousands of refugees crossed into Indian territory. Dalai Lama's exit further aggravated tension on both sides. Chinese believed that the Tibetan guerrillas were receiving arms from the Indian side of the border. The Chinese harboured the feeling that whatever little military build-up India had effected on the border was motivated by inherent hostility. Some of the documents which were

captured later during the crisis revealed the Chinese rulers' mind in giving instructions to military commanders that India in collaboration with the US was planning to launch a joint attack against Tibet. The military commanders were warned to keep a vigilant eye on the movements of Indian troops and avoid clashes with them.[7] It was at that time that China proposed that it would accept the Mc Mahon line in the east if India agreed to accept the Chinese claim for Aksai Chin region through which a strategically important road was constructed to join West Tibet with Sinkiang. India could read the motive of the proposal and rejected the offer.

The Soviet Union was also disturbed by the Tibetan uprising and the first precautionary step it took was the sudden establishment of an embassy in Kathmandu. Moscow came to realise that now onwards Peking would try to spread its influence in the Himalayan borderland. Due to physical distance and the position of Nepal as a landlocked country Soviet Union could not compete with China in trying to have upperhand in the politics of the Himalayan states. Nor did it want. Its basic objective was to see that the Soviet diplomatic pressure in Nepal would help Indian interests which were vital vis-a-vis China. To that extent the Chinese ambitions would be curbed and the Soviet Union benefited.

In January 1959, more than two months before the Lhasa uprising, Chou En-lai again repeated China's offer to accept the Mc Mahon line in return for India's recognition of China's title to Aksai Chin. But India could not agree to such a compromise which amounted to recognition of a territory captured surreptitiously. Now China started thinking that if India was made to accept the Chinese proposal stronger persuasion was necessary which could be possible in the form of a war. So China's invasion of India was intended to provide such 'persuasion'. In other words it was designed to confirm Indian fears that China was out to find a solution of the boundary problem through military action and to force India to negotiate the boundary issue on China's terms.

On 20 October the Chinese attacked on both sides of the border with such a huge force that within four days they occupied all the territory they claimed. On 24 October they called for a ceasefire to be followed by the withdrawal of troops on both sides from the line of actual control they had reached on 24 October. When India

did not respond they again attacked and marched further. Meanwhile, India had received adequate arms aid from friendly nations. There was also pressure on them from the Soviet side. All these factors compelled the Chinese to withdraw unilaterally. The main point of concern has been whether China should maintain their 24 October position or withdraw further to the position they had occupied before fighting broke out.

What is important is to note that at the time when we had suffered the disastrous loss of a full brigade consisting of the flowers of Indian army, India's representative at the UN, B.N. Chakarvarty, was pleading the cause of China for UN membership. His argument was, as usual, that by being a member of the world body China could be subjected to its views and discipline. This time the Afro-Asian bloc was not warm in supporting India as they could not find any rationale for such a preposterous plea. The Ugandan Prime Minister Obote openly refused to support China's candidacy until the shooting stopped. But India, for reasons which nobody could understand, continued to press for it.[8]

The Chinese surely felt unnerved by the unfavourable reactions which their aggression on India provoked. The keynote of their attitude was made public as early as January 1963 when East Germany's communist leader Walter Ulbricht in the presence of Khrushchev stated at the opening ceremony of the East German communist party's sixth conference that China invaded India without informing any fraternal communist government. He castigated Peking for not abiding by the principle of settlement through negotiations which was a basic tenet of peaceful coexistence.[9]

In the foreign communist circles it was assumed that China's attack on India was calculated to force the Soviet Union to repudiate the concept of peaceful coexistence and abandon its neutral stance in the Sino-Indian dispute. They knew that China would not be able to achieve either objective. They knew what Khrushchev had told a Chinese delegation headed by Teng Hsiao-peng in July 1963 that the Soviet Union and India 'stood side by side' on the problem of securing peace. The delegation was returning to China following the failure to patch-up ideological

split. The Chinese reaction to Khrushchev's remark was very bitter. They equated Moscow's India policy with the withdrawal of Soviet missiles from Cuba as true example of cowardice.

China's hostility towards India as witnessed in the aggression of 1962, more than any other single factor, made a farce of the five principles of peaceful coexistence signed in 1954 and wrecked the Bandung spirit so hopefully enunciated in April 1955 at Bandung, Indonesia. The second Bandung conference was scheduled to be held in November 1965 in Algiers, largely as a result of Chinese pressure. Peking wanted to exploit it to assert its leadership which it could do now as Nehru was there no more. But China's aggression on India in 1962, its abortive intrusion into Indo-Pak war in 1965 and its failure in instigating a pro-Peking communist coup in Indonesia which took place on the eve of the conference created an atmosphere in which China could not dare to pose itself as a potential leader of Afro-Asian nations. Moreover, the likelihood that the Soviet Union would be invited and would exploit it to malign China caused Peking to reverse its position and sabotage the meeting at the eleventh hour.[10]

It was an irony of the situation that the US and China should have found an identity of views on the Bangladesh crisis though on every other issue they differed widely. Apparently both were playing the same game which was to prevent two developments: disintegration of Pakistan and outbreak of war between India and Pakistan. With that end in view, both wanted a political solution of the problem but the solution should be accommodated within the existing frame work of Pakistan, that is without impairing the political unity of Pakistan. Chin, in his banquet speech in honour of Bhutto delegation on 7 November 1972 did not detail the kind of settlement China would regard as acceptable but the government spokesmen often did indicate that Peking stood behind the determination of the Pakistani government to bar the secession of the east wing.[11] Secondly, both the powers wanted a negotiated settlement of this issue but a settlement negotiated not between the elected representatives of Bangladesh and the military junta in West Pakistan, but between New Delhi and Islamabad. To this India could never agree as it was clearly a conflict between the two wings of Pakistan and it was for them to come to terms. How could India come in the picture? It may also be recalled that

Pakistan had already been clamouring for a negotiated settlement with India. Bhutto was understood to have said earlier in Peking that he favoured bilateral negotiations between India and Pakistan which would be held either under the auspices of the UN or even outside it. India had consistently opposed it for very valid reasons.

Another strange aspect of Sino-American attitude was that keeping aside all considerations of ideology, political morality and fairness of approach, both America and China came out openly to criticise India for interfering in the internal affairs of Pakistan. If the Chinese could claim the right to intervene in Korea and if the US could come thousands of miles away with all the military strength to protect the so-called democracy in Vietnam then why could not India take protective measures to ensure its social, economic and political structure which was being threatened by the massive influx of refugees and hundreds of saboteurs? Likewise, America could disregard the world public opinion in giving free reins to Israel to inflict death and devastation on the Arabs of West Asia but when India wanted to help the persecuted people in its neighbouring country, Washington was the first to come out with protests and threats.

Realising that their proposals would not be acceptable to India and also being conscious of the dangers of an outbreak of war between India and Pakistan, the next alternative of which both America and China could think was a stalemate over Bangladesh for a long time to come. Both felt that such a state would dissipate India's determination to shape the ultimate outcome in Bangladesh. They thought that intensity of Indian emotions would not last long and local pressure groups would demand India's disengagement from this crisis as it was unnecessarily straining its resources. Moreover, both the powers were under the impression that warmth of Indo-Soviet friendship which had encouraged India to be so bellicose would also cool down. The treaty which was hurriedly signed did not reflect any deep identity of views of the two signatories. It was just a make-shift arrangement made on the spur of the moment as a riposte to Sino-American move to detente.[12]

This is how US and China viewed the advantages of prolonging the crisis. The U.S. had another interest if the crisis was not resolved

soon. It would have given the Americans time to ensure that if and when an independent Bangladesh came into being theirs would be the dominant role in its creation. Americans, in that case, would do their best to see that even if East Bengal became independent for all practical purposes some sort of loose unity between the two wings would be maintained. Washington was particularly anxious that the new free Bengal would not be allowed to deviate from a foreign policy stance evolved over the years in Pakistan under their guidance and direct supervision since the creation of SEATO and CENTO alliances.

For the Chinese there was an additional reason in being happy if the crisis went on for an indefinite period. If India succeeded soon in helping Bangladesh to come into being as an independent state it would re-establish India's image as an important power in South Asia, an image badly mauled in the conflict with China in 1962. This China did not want; so it was interested in the prolongation of the crisis.

China felt helpless in not being able to exploit the turmoil to its own political advantage. Since it was committed to support Yahya Khan, China could not ask its followers to take the lead and capture the leadership of the movement. Maoists in East Bengal were expected to support Yahya because China was supporting him. Yahya's forces had spared the pro-China people while they were mercilessly killing others particularly Mujib's men and Hindus. China believed that if the crisis dragged on, the leadership of Bangladesh would pass into the hands of extremist elements deriving inspiration and even guidance from the Chinese.

China and America had another interest in wishing that the crisis was prolonged. India was already burdened with about ten million refugees, most of them being Hindus; both believed that the Muslim refugees might go back but Hindus would not return even if an independent Bangladesh came into being. Thus India would be saddled with a worry which it could not bear alone. To share this financial burden India would have to approach some other powers, America being one of them. In that case America would have a leverage to influence India. The two powers, America and China, believed that by putting pressure on the world powers India was trying to keep up the problems of these refugees alive.

Their presumption was that in the absence of India's support Mukti Bahini would have long been crushed by Pakistani army and so long as that support was available, Pakistani military rulers could not be persuaded to initiate moves towards an acceptable political settlement.

Verbally at least China's support for Pakistan military junta was more emphatic than that of the US but India did not take notice of it and hardly reacted as sharply as she had to the American attitude. Why? For the obvious reason that not much was expected from China by way of impartial understanding let alone support of any kind. This is also true that if New Delhi was much more shocked by the American attitude than by the Chinese this was partly because of the different diplomatic expectations from Washington and Peking and partly because Pakistan was emboldened not so much by the Chinese support as by the American.[13] But when Kissinger met Chinese leaders in Peking in July and October 1971, the Indian government felt a little apprehensive that both countries may formulate a common policy towards Bangladesh. It could not be reliably known what joint decision was taken by America and China at the time of Kissinger's visits to Peking but by the time he returned, it became apparent that the two sides had reached some agreement which was aimed both at the Soviet Union and its allies like India.

There were visible signs to strengthen such presumption. Till Kissinger's visit to Peking, America had adopted an ambivalent position on the Bangladesh issue but soon thereafter the US took up a tough anti-India position and gradually became increasingly hostile towards India. China also started talking against alleged Indian intervention in East Bengal and after the second visit of Kissinger in October the Chinese became all the more vehement in denouncing India for joining hands with the Soviet Union in exploiting the situation in Bangladesh. The Chinese seemed to be naive enough to have envisaged the liberation movement as nothing more than a manipulation of the Indian government and assumed that if it gained power, thanks to India's victory, it would be so beholden to India as not to be worthy of Chinese notice as an independent nation.[14]

2

BACKGROUND SURVEY

Though geographically near, China has been a distant land to India because of the Himalayas and the arid Tibetan plateau in the north and the dense jungles of Burma in the east. The main cause of cultural contacts with India was the introduction of Buddhism in China. What is remarkable about the potency of Buddhist faith was that it found ready acceptance at the Chinese hands even when Confucius, a contemporary of Buddha, was preaching his new faith among the Chinese people. To probe into the depths of what was a new faith for them, a number of Chinese scholars came to India and Indian missionaries went to China to create wider contacts with the people there. The most famous among the Chinese who came to India were Fa-Shien, Hsuan-Tsang and Yun-Tsiang. Among the Indians who went to China were Kashyap Matango, Kumarjin and Gunavala. The Chinese scholars not only studied Buddhism, but also translated several scriptures in their language and carried with them hundreds of manuscripts. The Indian scholars mostly did the preaching work explaining in the Chinese language, the basic tenets of Buddhism which could be accepted and implemented among the Chinese people without prejudice to the ancient values which they had preserved in their social life. This interchange of moral values among the people of the two countries remains the most important fact in the history of world civilizations.

These contacts relapsed into forgetfulness probably on account of vicissitudes of life and changes in circumstances. The regional

contacts and continental pressures kept the two countries striving to survive with their ancient past and left no time for them to renew their old interests. Physical contacts were debarred by high Himalayas on one hand and by the far flung sea routes on the other.

However, whenever opportunity arose it was utilized for developing mutual contacts. The visit of Tagore to China in 1924 marked the resumption of old national relationship between the two countries. The impression that he created was akin to that of the sages in the past. The simple Chinese people generally regarded Tagore and Gandhi as the modern Buddhas of India. It found expression in the establishment of China Bhawan in Santiniketan in 1934 and of a Sino-Indian cultural society in Nanking in 1941 with the object of linking up the cultural values of the two countries.

Nehru visited China in August 1939 when it was engaged in a fierce war with Japan. During his speeches he talked of 'imperishable links' which kept the two countries together for ages which he hoped would revive in a more coherent form when an 'eastern federation of India and China would take form'. Soon thereafter two Chinese goodwill missions led by two leading Chinese figures Tai Chi-Tao and Rev Tiu Hsu came to India. Dr. S. Radhakrishnan responded these visits by giving a series of lectures in China from 7-21 May 1941. He talked of 'our civilizations possessing a common cultural and spiritual background' with an identity of 'ideas of happy life and friendship'. 'As good neighbours they are a model for others', he stressed.

Indian leaders have always been highly critical of the manner in which various Western powers tore up China to advance their own economic and strategic interests. The sufferings and humiliation of a proud people belonging to a great civilization and culture became an emotive concern of the Indian sentiments. They pledged full support to the Chinese people in their heroic struggle against foreign invaders, hailed the opium wars and Boxer revolt (1889-90) and expressed solidarity with the anti-imperialist forces in China. In the 1930s when Japan invaded Manchuria (1932) occupied Jehol (1933) and declared war on China (July 1937) Indian opinion all over the country was greatly agitated so much so that

each section contributed its mite in concrete terms to condemn Japan, ranging from holding meetings and mass demonstrations to banning all Japanese goods from being used in Indian homes. In Santiniketan, Tagore closed down Japan Bhawan as an expression of his personal indignation over the spread of 'military nationalism in Asia'.[15] A medical mission was sent to China as a gesture of goodwill of Indian people towards patriotic Chinese who were in the midst of a grim struggle for their survival. The bonds of friendship grew further with the visit of Chiang Kai-shek and his wife to India in 1942. Chiang supported India's cause for freedom and conveyed a warning to President Roosevelt that the British policy in India had to be reviewed so that India's support may be enlisted to ensure the allied victory over the Axis powers.

In India we had a Sinophil in Nehru. Mahatma Gandhi during his talks with Chiang was reported to have referred to Nehru's visit to China in 1939. 'After that visit', Gandhi said 'Nehru had returned home with a love for your country, excelled, if at all, by his love of his own country'. Such sentiments and personal bonds did not pave the way for an objective understanding of Chinese developments, especially in regard to the issues of civil war between the KMT and communist forces. Nehru's personal friendship with Chiang obsessed the correct vision of what was happening in China during and after the war. He continued to view the KMT leaders to be in the vanguard of nationalist movement even when the Chinese communists had established paramountcy in the anti-Japanese war.

During the period of civil war when the communist threat to the Chiang government became very serious Sen We Te-Chen who had become KMT's foreign minister in early 1944 summoned the envoys of Burma, Thailand, the Philippines and India and formally proposed an alliance to fight communism in their respective regions. Indian ambassador K.M. Panikkar conveyed this plan to the home government. It was immediately rejected and there ended the matter.[16]

After the communist take over, the goodwill that China got in ample measure in India as a result of the Japanese aggression had gone. The fall of Chiang was regretted in some political circles which recalled the support he had extended to the Indian liberation movement. But the general attitude towards the advent of

communist regime was neither alarmist nor naively optimistic. The Indian government tried to understand the new China and wanted to give it a chance to develop its domestic and international policies. In its view its outright rejection would be a diplomatic error. China wanted peace as much as India wanted for economic reconstruction and development; the maintenance of friendship with China was essential no matter what the government was in power. This is how the Indian government led by Nehru thought of the new China.

For his part, Nehru made an all out effort, to remove misgivings from the Chinese mind by offering them his country's goodwill in abundance. He exulted in China's recovery and resurgence, gave them an honourable place among the newly independent Asian nations and strove hard to secure for China its rightful place among the nations of the world. India became the stoutest non-communist champion of China in the international fora. Every year India took the lead in pursuing Peking's claim to China seat in the UN in the face of strong opposition from a number of non-communist countries. Nehru repeatedly pleaded for the restoration of Formosa and the offshore islands to communist China. He initiated the exchange of a series of cultural and technical missions with China to promote friendship between the two countries. Finally, in April 1954 India concluded a treaty with China in terms of which India renounced all the rights and privileges which it had inherited from the British.

For reasons which even his colleagues could not understand. Nehru refused to take a grim view of the Chinese takeover of Tibet. He deplored the use of force by China against Tibet but he claimed that friendship and not opposition was the way to divert the Chinese into right channel and prevent them from going into wrong ones. Again, when the Tibetan issue came before the UN, with the help of the British, whose interest in India had by then become only secondary, India scotched the debate on Tibetan question in the UN Security Council.

China's occupation of Tibet was in itself an expression of callousness towards a very delicate issue but the intemperate language which was used in Chinese notes amounted to adding insult to injury. Despite the reverses, India continued to maintain a dignified approach which was prominently displayed during the

Korean crisis in 1950. Initially India had voted in favour of UN action against North Korea but when the Chinese entered in the war at the end of the year, India resisted the US move to condemn China as an aggressor by the General Assembly as it would enlarge the area of hostilities. In its efforts to bring about a settlement, Indian government served as a channel of communication of Chinese intentions and requirements to the outside world and pursued vigorously for the recognition of China as the rightful representative of Chinese seat in the UN. In September 1951, India declined to attend the conference at San Francisco for the conclusion of a peace treaty with Japan because among other reasons, China was not a party to it.

3

EMERGENCE OF COMMUNIST CHINA

In 1947, when India became independent, China was in the midst of civil war. To set up diplomatic contacts with her, India did not wait for the day when normalcy would prevail there. India sent its first ambassador to China in April 1948. Ambassador Panikkar's assignment to China in the last days of the KMT regime was mainly to assess and report on the nature of calibre of communist leadership which was going to assume power soon. This he did in his long reports to Nehru personally. By the middle of 1949 it became clear that China was going communist and there was no power to reverse the process. Now the question of recognition was before the government. Krishna Menon had already started negotiations with the British government but the latter seemed to be indecisive. This caused some delay in India's decision which, however, came on 30 December 1949 after the nationalist government had moved to Taiwan. India was next to Burma, in being the non-communist country to accord recognition to China. India's prompt recognition of the Chinese communist government and withdrawal of the recognition from the Chiang Kai-shek government did not evoke any favourable response from Peking. Both the actions of the government of India were taken for granted and derogatory references to India and its policies continued to appear in the Chinese press.

When on 1 October 1949, China was declared a people's

republic, the communist party of India congratulated Mao for this achievement. Mao in his characteristic style assured that '...relying on the brave communist party of India, India will certainly not remain for long under the yoke of imperialism'. Mao assured Indian communists that 'like free China a free India will one day emerge in the socialist and democratic family.'[17] The key note was struck in 1949-50 when communist China showed complete contempt for India's capitalist democratic system. Nehru was branded, 'a running dog of imperialism'. A Chinese editorial lumped Nehru with Bio Dai, Syngman Rhee and Chiang Kai-shek as among the 'dregs of mankind'. [18] As regards Indian policy of nonalignment, it had always remained suspect in Chinese eyes. Mao in this connection remarked, 'to sit on the fence is impossible... as everywhere in the world one either leans to the side of imperialism or to the side of socialism'. Neutrality to him was 'a mere camouflage and third world does not exist'.[19]

China from the very beginning looked towards India with a sense of superority. After assuming charge of the Indian embassy in Peking, K.M. Panikkar lost no time in understanding that his hosts looked at his country very much in a condescending or superior manner. They seemed to be friendly towards India but were inclined to be a little patronizing. Panikkar described this was the KMT attitude also which did not change even after the communist takeover of the Chinese government. On the other hand, it seemed to have been hardened in view of Chinese having attained the status of a great power in the context of post-war world developments.

As an illustration, Nehru's experience in this connection makes a very painful reading. When he visited China in 1954 he was supposed to pay a courtesy call on Mao Tse-tung which he did. But he was made to feel as if he was being ushered in as some one coming from a tributory or vassal state of the Chinese empire.[20] On a subsequent occasion Liu Shao-chi had told Vietnam leaders in 1962 that the Chinese could never accept India's attitude that it was a great power nor could they tolerate the Indians feeling themselves superior to the Chinese.

All this happened at the time when India was making an all out effort to befriend China. But China, on its part, continued to

harbour basic contradictions between Indian objectives and Chinese global aims and long term strategy to achieve them. The enormous output of the communist daily press from 1951 to 1957 when relations between the two countries were at the best, often made references to the exchange of diplomatic or cultural missions of diverse kinds between China and other countries but seldom did they make any serious, let alone sympathetic, discussion of either India's internal affairs or external policies.

At the Bandung conference in 1955 Chou En-lai was not regarded by several small states of Asia as a welcome participant. Each had its own tale to tell, may be against the vagaries of overseas Chinese or against the great power complex on the part of China which later caused conflict in Vietnam and Indonesia. It is there that Nehru introduced Chou En-lai to other delegates in extremely complimentary terms to dispel their fears of China and bring China out of its isolation. To some Chinese it appeared as if Nehru was quite openly trying to take Chou under his wings disregarding perhaps naively the implications of superiority that this apparent kindliness must carry.[21]

Indians may have regarded this as one more incident meriting Chinese gratitude but to the Chinese it seemed to have appeared as the height of presumption. Chou was reported to have often felt irritated when he recollected this incident. He recalled the incident to Pakistani journalists in China in 1965 while commenting on Nehru's arrogance, and at about the same time told some visiting Ceylonese politicians, 'I have never met a more arrogant man than Nehru'.[22] To what extent Nehru was arrogant would be clear from what he had said about Chou En-lai. Once referring to Chou to an august gathering in India Nehru had no hesitation in asking them with enthusiasm: 'Is he not a great gentleman'.[23]

With reference to the same occasion, it may be recalled that Pakistan had objected to China being invited to Bandung and so did the U.K. Oddly enough it was at Bandung that the China-Pak entente was first forged in secret talks between Chou En-lai and Mohammad Ali Bogra, Pak Prime Minister. For the record, it may be recalled that Pakistan was a member of SEATO which was essentially directed against Chinese threat to SEA as viewed by America then. According to Professor Rushbrook Williams, Chou

told his Pak counterpart that there was 'no conceivable clash of interests which could imperil friendly relations' between the two countries. As if to underline the point the Chinese leader was reported to have added, 'this was not true of relations between India and China' and that 'a definite conflict of interests between them could be expected soon'. In retrospect, how one wished Nehru had his ear to the ground and his feet too on firm soil with a close tab on reality. Writing in 1966, a Pakistani academic noted that while Bandung marked the end of the Sino-Indian honeymoon, it also marked the beginning of understanding between Pakistan and China.[24]

In recapitulation it should be specifically stated in brief that after extending recognition, India consistently tried to cultivate friendship with China. This was quite clear from the several steps that India took like (i) the repeated resolutions sponsored by Indian delegations to the UN urging that the People's government should represent China in the UN, (ii) the exchange of state visits by the Prime Ministers of India and China, (iii) visits of numerous cultural delegations from India to China and vice-versa, (iv) the trade agreement between India and China on 14 October 1954, (v) participation in industrial and other exhibitions, (vi) the visits of technical experts to China from India to study such subjects as agrarian conditions and the like and (vii) the establishment and promotion of India-China friendship association in both countries.[25]

Other indications of India's desire to be friendly with China were: (i) India voted against a resolution in the General Assembly of the UN branding China as an aggressor in Korea, (ii) India declined to attend a conference convened at San Francisco in 1951 to sign a peace treaty with Japan because among other reasons, China was not a party to it, and India felt that attending an important conference on the Far East, with China left out, would not be fair to China and (iii) in 1953 India introduced a resolution in the General Assembly of the UN on the question of the prisoners of war; Nehru declared that the resolution was intended to accommodate the view point of China, as far as possible, on the question. [26] However, China did not seem to have understood the significance of India's gesture of goodwill towards her. When the massive Chinese intervention in Korea in November 1950 succeeded in driving back the UN forces to the 38th parallel, India's

representative at the UN B.N. Rau, with the support of fourteen other Afro-Asian countries issued an appeal to China not to cross the 38th parallel. The appeal was direct and sincere and gave the first indication that the Afro-Asian countries had taken the initiative to prevent the escalation of conflict in the Far East which might ultimately envelop the entire world. Chinese were also expected to view this gesture gracefully, but they reacted violently calling the Afro-Asian resolution 'illegal' and a 'trick'.

But all this seemed to have been a one-sided effort. China in response continued to remain indifferent to the spirit with which India undertook these steps. When on 21 October 1950, the government of India drew the attention of the government of China to the harmful effects of resorting to military action to 'liberate' Tibet as such action might lead to the disturbances on India's borders, they received a rude reply criticising the government of India 'as having been affected by foreign influences hostile to China in Tibet'.[27]

4

TIBETAN PROBLEM

The Tibetan problem had already been there even before the communists took over China. The KMT government was as firm as its communist successors in considering Tibet as a part of China. Chiang Kai-shek got annoyed when he came to know that a Tibetan delegation had visited India in 1948. His government sought assurance that 'Indian dealings with the Tibetan mission would not, in any way, be detrimental to the sovereignty and territorial integrity of China'. Chiang was assured by K.P.S. Menon, the then Indian envoy, that there was no such intention on the part of the Indian government.[28] The mission visited Washington and London and arrived in Nanking in April 1949 where they were described as a delegation to the National Assembly. Communist armies were then sweeping across China and no follow-up was made by Chiang. Meanwhile, the Tibetan government dismissed all Chinese officials associated with Chiang's government, took over the radio station and forbade all communications with China. The Tibetan government apprehended that with the collapse of the Chinese nationalist government, the members of the Chinese bureaucracy might transfer their allegiance to the communist government and the Tibetan government would then be faced with an established communist foothold in their country.

The communist march went on relentlessly so much so that by 1 October 1949 the entire country collapsed under communist rule. But on that occasion no reference was made to Tibet. Two months later, on 1 January 1950, the liberation of Tibet was officially

announced as one of the main tasks of the people's liberation army. It appeared clear that China wanted to enforce its authority over Tibet; Indian government, through its ambassador in Peking expressed the hope that the Tibetan issue would be peacefully settled and that Tibet would continue to enjoy the autonomy that it had enjoyed so far. This the Indian government formally did on 24 August 1950 through an official communication. To this the Chinese reply was that while the liberation of Tibet was a sacred duty, the Chinese government was anxious to secure their ends by negotiations and not by military means.[29]

However, the Lhasa National Assembly, meeting in an extraordinary session recognized the need to seek outside help and made preparations to send diplomatic mission to some countries like USA, UK, India and Nepal to plead Tibet's case. The Chinese gave, in general terms, a strong warning that acceptance of 'illegal' diplomatic mission by any country would be considered a hostile act towards China. Apparently, this had some effect on the western countries which refused to receive Tibetan mission. India was also not prepared to incur Chinese displeasure or risk its new approach towards China by receiving a Tibetan delegation which had assumed a sovereign posture.

In addition to the announcement the Chinese made on 1 January 1950, they also proposed to hold a meeting in Peking of 'Tibetan demographic personages' to discuss problems of Tibet. Lhasa reconciled to the idea that if any autonomy was to be retained it would have to be the result of direct negotiations with Peking. But Lhasa wanted the talks to be held on neutral ground especially in Hongkong where the Chinese pressure would be less. The Tibetan delegation was held up in India enroute to Hongkong because the British authorities prevaricated in issuing visas to them. The British authorities apparently felt that the delicacy of Hongkong's political position made it undesirable to allow communist China and Tibet to hold any talks in that colony.[30]

However, the talks began in New Delhi in September 1950 with the new Chinese ambassador who had recently assumed charge of his office. In Chinese view such important negotiations could not be held at a distant foreign place like Delhi; they immediately insisted that the Tibetan delegation moved to Peking. It seemed

that the Chinese had felt that Nehru was over reaching himself in delaying, for well over a year, the negotiations between Dalai Lama's representatives and the Chinese leadership. It was too much for them to see negotiations over the future of Tibet being conducted in Delhi under the auspices of the government of India.[31]

When intimated that further talks could take place only in Peking, the Tibetan delegation left New Delhi for Calcutta on its way to Peking on 25 October. But before the last leg of its journey could commence, events had completely over taken it, for on 7 October the Chinese army had marched into Tibet and less than a fortnight later Chando, an important town in the eastern Tibet had fallen to its advance guards. All this was not confirmed for another few days. The Indian ambassador K.M. Panikkar tried to get some definite information but the most he could wring out of the Chinese sources was that certain pacificatory measures were taken in West Sinkiang that was on the border of Tibet proper. It was confirmed on 25 October by the announcement on the Peking radio that the process of liberating Tibet had begun. This happened a day after the Chinese forces had entered Korea to check the UN forces who were going to reach towards North Korea crossing the 38th parallel. Thus the two military operations began almost simultaneously.

During the period negotiations were going on with the Tibetans, the Chinese had made all the preparations to launch an attack on Tibet, as well as to face the UN forces in Korea. Due to the state of poor communication, deep forests and extremely rough terrain the Chinese advance in later stages was very slow. The Chinese version was that the military operation was in the nature of military pressure on the Tibetan government to force the latter to accept the Chinese sovereignty. It was with this end in view that the Chinese after their initial military display preferred to keep the armies on the frontier and press the Tibetans to go to Peking for negotiations. The main reason was that China wanted to know the reactions of the so-called 'imperialists' including India. If a violent protest had been made, China would have taken the plea that it had conquered that part of inner China that the Dalai Lama had illegally occupied under British instigation in 1931 when China was weak. At that time the question of China's admission to the UN was pending; China was anxious to know how the public opinion in the UN was viewing its adventures in Tibet.

On 8 October the UN forces in Korea crossed north of the 38 parallel despite India's repeated warnings that China would enter the war if this happened. Now the war had assumed fierce proportions compelling India to plunge itself into the vortex of crucial negotiations to prevent the conflict from becoming the third world war which would have been an unprecedented catastrophe. While India was busy in the peace mission, China invaded Tibet. This unprovoked aggression on the part of China came as a great shock to India but in the larger interests of world peace India remained busy with the Korean war giving comparatively less attention to Tibet. Thus the danger of a world conflict developing out of the Korean war eclipsed the threat posed by the invasion of Tibet. Even if India had supported the Tibetan cause, it would have greatly irritated China without any good being achieved. China's representative a General Wu arrived at the UN towards the end of November. Indian delegate B.N. Rau was instructed to hold talks with Wu to explore all possibilities for a peaceful settlement. The way had to be cleared for the vital negotiations and this could be done only when India did not give any threat to China on Tibetan issue.

On 21 October 1950, the Indian ambassador delivered to the Chinese government a memorandum expressing India's concern over China taking military action against Tibet. Indian government's main argument was that it was the time when the opinion in the UN was gradually going in favour of China's admission to the world body. China's military move on the eve of the session of the UN General Assembly would give powerful support to those countries who were opposed to the entry of China in the UN. In brief, India appealed mainly to China's self-interest rather than showing concern for its own well-established rights in Tibet. It also ignored the right of the Tibetan people as well as the principle of self determination which India had always championed. Again, the need for a peaceful solution was emphasized in terms of China's long range objectives in the attainment of which peaceful solution of Tibetan problem would contribute a great deal besides laying down a healthy precedent to solve such a crucial issue.

In another note dated 28 October 1950, the government of India repeated the reasons why the Tibetan delegation could not proceed

to Peking immediately to start negotiations there. Besides their inability to get a visa, their lack of knowledge on how to deal with other countries and the necessity of obtaining instructions from their government, who in turn had to consult their National Assembly, caused some more delay. But it was made clear that no foreign influence hostile to China had been responsible for the delay in departure of the Tibetan delegation. China was also told that in the midst of war, no peaceful negotiations with the Tibetans could be possible as it would clearly mean to them that negotiations were being held under duress. In view of these considerations, invasion of Tibet by Chinese troops could only be regarded as deplorable, not being in the interest of China or of peace.

The Chinese in their note dated 31 October said that the problem of Tibet was entirely the domestic problem of China and no foreign interference would be tolerated. The Chinese army must enter Tibet to liberate it and defend the frontiers of China. It accused the Tibetan delegation of intentionally delaying the date of its departure to Peking; this, the Chinese held, they did under external instigation. The Chinese clearly told India to be aware of the fact that the problem of Tibet and the problem of the participation of China in the UN were two extremely separate problems each had nothing to do with the other. Finally, India's statement that Chinese armed intervention in Tibet was deplorable was affected by foreign influences hostile to China.

In its response, the government of India firmly denied that their previous representation was affected by any foreign source inimical to China. India's policy in this matter was totally independent, solely directed towards the peaceful settlement of the dispute under reference. The government also denied that Tibetan delegation's departure was delayed by external instigation. The government of India had sought earnestly that a settlement of the Tibetan problem should be effected by peaceful negotiations adjusting the legitimate Tibetan claim to autonomy within the framework of China's suzerainty. India had no political or historical ambitions towards Tibet and did not seek any more privileged position for themselves or for their nationals.

The Chinese response dated 16 November repeated their earlier allegations about the deliberate delay the Tibetan delegation had

caused in reaching Peking for peaceful negotiations. They should have reached there by mid-September which date was further extended up to the end of month. The Chinese could no longer continue to put off their set plan of the Chinese army proceeding to Tibet as the Tibetans continued to fabricate various pretexts to postpone their departure. The Chinese note criticized India for disregarding the facts of the case and regarding a domestic problem of the Chinese government—the exercise of its sovereign rights in Tibet—as an international dispute calculated to increase the present deplorable tension in the world.

In the course of exchange of notes, India's case was categorically made clear which could be stated briefly as follows: (i) India throughout remained a powerful advocate of peaceful negotiations to resolve the differences between Tibet and China: (ii) India supported the legitimate Tibetan claims to autonomy within the framework of Chinese suzerainty; (iii) India never meant to interfere in China's internal affairs; whatever India suggested in this connection was a well meant advice of a friendly country; (iv) India had no political or economic interests much less to retain some extra-territorial rights that it had acquired in Tibet during the British regime; (v) India was opposed to a military action in Tibet as it was in the interest of none including China.

As a reaction to India's opposition to China's action in Tibet in 1950. the Chinese invited an unofficial Indian delegation to China on the occasion of May day celebrations in 1951. The delegation consisted of those people who were supposed to speak in a language which would be pleasing to the Chinese ear. The government of India pointed out to the impropriety of the procedure in inviting the delegation without reference to the ministry of external affairs. As a matter of protocol procedure the invitation should have been routed through the government of India. In response, the Chinese agreed to receive an official delegation. In May 1952, the government sent a goodwill mission led by Mrs. Pandit. Later, to return this visit the Chinese sent an official cultural delegation to India.[32]

TIBETAN ISSUES IN THE UN

During the course of negotiations, Tibetan leadership requested

Indian government to sponsor its case in the UN. Indian response was that it should make a direct appeal to that world body. On 7 November 1950, a Tibetan delegation staying in Kalimpong appealed to the UN to come to its rescue against the armed invasion of Tibet by China. It specifically referred to the Simla convention of 1914 at which Tibet accepted nominal Chinese suzerainty conditionally and stated that the invasion of Tibet for its incorporation in communist China through sheer physical force was a clear case of aggression. Tibetans were basically and culturally quite different from the Chinese and as such they had a right to maintain their entity. The memorandum further said that before running over the country by force the correct course for the Chinese should have been to ascertain the Tibetan peoples' views by some civilized method like plebiscite whether they wanted to get integrated into China or remain an independent state.

The response from the UN was very disappointing. When the onslaught by the advancing Chinese forces became irresistible, Dalai Lama decided to appeal for help to the UN. But since Tibet was not a member of the Organisation, he appealed to India to sponsor his country's case. But the government of India advised him to send Tibet's appeal direct to the UN headquarters. Dalai Lama was still hopeful of India's support as he continued to remind himself of what Gopalaswamy Ayyangar, then railway minister and a member of the foreign affairs committee of the cabinet had said about this issue. He was reported to have said: 'according to our present judgement on the question and its merit we are prepared to support Tibet's case in the UN to the extent that China should have solved this question by peaceful means and it was wrong of her to have marched her armies into Tibet for settling the question'.[33]

However, Tibet found a sponsor in a small Latin American country, El Salvador who proposed that when the appeal came, the General Assembly should take up this issue on 24 November 1950. But when the appeal came for consideration the British representative who was the first to speak on the issue said that as the leagal position of Tibet was not clear, it would be better if the matter was allowed to wait till the Assembly had a better idea of the possibilities of a peaceful settlement. India was relieved that

now it would have no chance to offend China. Its delegate in the UN supported the British proposal on the plea that the Chinese in an official communication had assured the government of India that the Chinese had ceased to advance after the fall of Chando, a town about 480 km. east of Lhasa. He further hoped that the Tibetan issue would be settled by peaceful means. In the view of the government of India the best way to attaining that objective was to abandon the idea of including that question on the agenda of the General Assembly.

An event be noted in this connection. At the UN Headquarters, the same day when the Tibetan issue came for discussion, the Chinese communist delegation which had been invited to the UN to present a complaint against the alleged US aggression in the Taiwan area, presented their credentials to the UN. The presence of the Chinese delegation gave the UN a chance to negotiate informally with them on the Korean crisis but it distracted attention from the Tibetan problem. Tibet became very much a side issue.

Again on 12 October 1959 the UN General Assembly took up for consideration its earlier recommendation to include the question of Tibet in the agenda. India's representative abstained from voting for two reasons which Nehru had earlier made in Parliament. He had said that the UN could not accuse China of violating human rights in Tibet as the former was not allowed to be the member of the UN. Secondly, Tibet had not been acknowledged as an independent state for considerable time and because of this reason it could not become a member of the UN. This point was contested by Dalai Lama who reminded Nehru of what he had said a year ago about the status of Tibet. Reminding Peking of about the Simla convention of 1904 Nehru had said 'this was not the first time that Tibet conducted treaties in her own rights. There at the Simla convention Tibetan and the Chinese plenipotentiaries met on an equal footing. But about the latter statement of Nehru questioning the independent status of Tibet, Dalai said: 'if you deny sovereign status to Tibet, you deny the validity of the Simla convention and therefore the validity of the McMahon line'. This statement quite understandably angered Nehru.

As a result of the UN decision, Tibetans now felt totally betrayed by all the socalled upholders of human rights. The Tibetans now

had no option left but to carry on negotiations with the Chinese, despite the humiliation they would suffer in the process. On 21 April 1951, the Tibetan government sent a delegation to Peking. This delegation joined the other one which had been delayed in India. It reached there on 26 April. The negotiations began on 29 April 1951 and concluded on 21 May. On 23 May an agreement was signed what was popularly known as the 17-point agreement.

The agreement sealed China's complete control over Tibet. To start with, Article 1 declared that the Tibetan people should unite and drive out imperialist aggressive forces from Tibet. It was difficult to discover who these imperialist forces were in Tibet. It was an attempt at shadow boxing against an imaginary enemy which could, in this case, be India alone. The main point in this agreement was that it enjoined the Tibetan people to return to the big family of motherland—the People's Republic of China. Tibet now stood completely integrated with the rest of China as a satellite state losing all semblance of autonomy. Article 2 asked the local Tibetan government to assist the people's liberation army to enter Tibet and consolidate the national defence. Article 8 laid down the reorganization of the Tibetan army and its integration with the Chinese army. Thus the Chinese got the legal authority to bring in an unrestricted number of troops into Tibet. China exploited this article to its maximum advantage. It went on increasing its forces in Tibet till the strength reached the peak figure of fourteen divisions in 1962. In the absence of such an agreement if China had taken any precipitate action it would have found an adverse resolution in the UN that would have further weakened its case to enter the UN. India also would have watched helplessly the possibility of its advocacy for China being exposed to ridicule and mockery.

Though autonomy was assured in Article 3, it could be exercised subject to the policies of the unified leadership of the Chinese government. The status, functions and powers of Dalai Lama and Panchen Lama were kept in the realm of religious affairs. To keep the religious susceptibilities of the people undisturbed some measures of reforms were announced such as the freedom of religion, preservation of the existing political system and protection of Tibetan language. Above all, economic reforms for the development of the country's national resources were loudly

announced. All this was done not after the negotiations between two equal participants in which discussions were free but in the midst of circumstances in which the Chinese were in a position to dictate and the Tibetans at the receiving end.

How did this agreement affect Indian interests? The agreement made no reference to India or to Indo-Tibetan relations except in a somewhat indirect and veiled one, 'assuring neighbouring countries' of the establishment and development of fair commercial and trading relations. For India the question was: would the new relationship between India and Tibet involve any change or modification of the rights and privileges which India or her agents enjoyed in Tibet? The government gave no explanation; it simply said in a statement issued on 15 September 1952 that the Indian mission in Lhasa would henceforth be designated as consulate general with three agencies at Gyantse, Gantok and Yatung under his supervision. The change in status resulted from the fact that the foreign relations of Tibet would now be conducted by China. It was plain that the government of India had now conceded the Chinese claim that Tibet did not enjoy the right to deal directly with her neighbours and that in that country and her autonomy we had no interests whatsoever apart from the small overland trade we carried.[34] The new position was clearly a reversal of the stand which the government of India had taken in 1950 namely that they had a national interest in the solution of problems affecting Tibet. However, the Indian government had several times stated their willingness to have Indian interests adjusted in the light of the changed circumstances.

5

1954 AGREEMENT

So long as the Chinese remained embroiled in Korean war and needed India's support they recognized the legitimacy of our trade and cultural interests in Tibet but as things improved a bit on the war front they started saying that the privileges that India enjoyed in Tibet were as a result of unequal treaties forced by the British on the unwilling but weak China. India had already agreed to the modification of some of the practices which had grown up in the past and to remove those which affected China's dignity. When peace was partly restored in Korea in mid-1953, China started taking action against the Indian position in Tibet. They objected to the despatch of fresh Indian troops to replace the guards at Gyantse and Yatung and seized the wireless set of the Indian trade agent at Gantok and prevented him from proceeding to the trade marts at Rudok and Taklakot. The Chinese would not allow the political officer in Sikkim to visit Lhasa except on a proper visa. The Prime Minister brought these happenings to the notice of Chinese Premier who considered as correct the actions taken by the Chinese officials in respect of events that Nehru had stated in his communications. Chou suggested that all the matters relating to India's right in Tibet required fresh review by both India and China. For this he proposed a meeting which should be held in Peking in December 1953.

In this context another incident should also be stated. Immediately after the communists took over Sinkiang, they forbade India's trade in that area. India had traditionally

maintained a consulate-general in Kashgar, capital city of Sinkiang for purposes of carrying trade between Kashmir and Sinkiang through Ladakh. On 8 December 1953, Nehru informed the Parliament that the Kashgar consulate would not be on the agenda of the forthcoming negotiations with China because the latter considered Sinkiang a closed area. As it became clear later, China not only refused India permission to reopen its Kashgar office but demanded the right to open three new Chinese trade missions in India. It was probably because the traditional Sino-Soviet competition for control of Sinkiang had entered a dangerous phase and that this was an important reason to keep India out of the area.[35]

The conference between the officials of the two countries opened in Peking on 31 December 1953 and dragged on for four months. The agreement was signed on 29 April 1954 and ratified on 3 June. India proposed that the agreement should last for twenty-five years but the Chinese reduced it to eight. In some political circles it was surmised that the signing of our accord was so timed by the Chinese that it should end just before the Prime Ministers of Colombo powers completed their deliberations—a coincidence which gave rise to speculation that China wanted to give evidence of its reasonableness.[36] The successful conclusion of negotiations was also linked with the opening of the Geneva conference on Indo-China where China could benefit from India's goodwill and the euphoric atmosphere created by the accord. If this was China's motive it was realized.

As for India, it sought a treaty agreement with China at this time when it had become a matter of common knowledge that the US was planning to extend military assistance to Pakistan. From November 1953, Indo-US relations deteriorated in anticipation of the US arms aid to boost Pakistan's military programme although the exact information was not formally announced until February 1954.

The preamble of the agreement contained the five principles of Panchsheel which both sides were supposed to observe in their mutual relationship but which later became the first victim of Chinese aggression in October 1962. They were: (1) mutual respect for each other's territorial integrity and sovereignty; (2) mutual

non-aggression; (3) mutual non-interference in each other's internal affairs; (4) equality and mutual benefit; and (5) mutual coexistence. During the visit of Chou En-lai the word 'mutual' in the articles concerned was omitted in the official communique issued on 20 June 1954 probably with a view to making them applicable to wider international context going much beyond the Sino-Indian relationship.

Nehru had earlier suggested that these principles should constitute a separate agreement so as to serve as guidelines in the light of which relations between any two countries with different political systems would be conducted peacefully. But the Chinese did not endorse this suggestion and proposed that they may be the part of some other major agreement. And this later had come to assume a secondary position in the form of a preamble of Sino-Indian agreement on Tibet. Even as an introductory part of the bigger agreement it did not seem to be either relevant or discreet. The main point of the agreement dealt with some specific issue which the two countries had to settle in the context of India having inherited some extra territorial rights in Tibet since the days of the British government and China having emerged as a strong unified power aspired to rule over Tibet as a matter of historical right.

Under the agreement were the right to station an Indian political agent at Lhasa, the right to maintain trade agencies at Gyantse, Gantok and Yatung as well as post and telegraph offices along the trade route up to Gyantse and finally the right to maintain military escorts at Yatung and Gyantse for the protection of Indian trade agencies as well as of the trade routes. The new treaty obliged India to transform its political agency at Lhasa into a consulate general, withdraw its military escort from Tibet and surrender all the communication installations to the Chinese government. These installations were to be handed over to China on the payment of a 'reasonable price'. But on the day following the signing of the treaty the government of India instructed the ambassador Raghavan that the postal telegraph and telephone installation together with equipment operated by India in Tibet were to be transferred free of cost and without compensation, to the Chinese government as a gesture of goodwill. India also gave China one more trading post in India in addition to the two already existing. China pressed

for one at Almora or Simla; India gave it at New Delhi instead. In return for our gesture of goodwill we had hoped that we might be permitted by China to reopen our consulate at Kashghar (Sinkiang). The Chinese government repeated the old statement that Sinkiang was a closed area.

By another article, India was allowed to maintain trade agencies in those three towns, Yatung, Gyantse and Gantok in which they have been functioning for long. China got in return the right to have trade agencies at New Delhi, Calcutta and Kalimpong, this being a new facility which China never had before. Likewise, India was given the right to set up trade marts at Yatung, Gyantse and Phari in central Tibet in view of similar facilities China would have in Kalimpong, Siliguri and Calcutta. As a result of these negotiations India retained what it had and China got some new concessions. But the Chinese refused to discuss the question of providing trade marts for Ladakhi traders in Western Tibet on the ground that this would involve a place in Kashmir which was under dispute between India and Pakistan. This seemed to be an attempt on the part of China to pose a neutralist position on a controversial issue in the politics of the subcontinent. Likewise, the Chinese refused to recognize the customary trade mart in Rudok (West Tibet) giving no valid reason for their refusal but obviously because China was building a road in Aksai Chin which passed through this town.

As earlier stated, under the treaty India agreed to regard Tibet as part of the sovereign territory of China and readily gave up all the rights it had inherited from the British. In some quarters it was regarded as a spectacular achievement of Asian statesmanship and Nehru believed that all problems left by history between India and China had for all time been successfully solved. But subsequent events falsified these sentiments and revealed a new facet of Chinese diplomacy marked by ruthless realism in which idealism and altruism had no place. It consolidated Chinese legal status of Tibet vis-a-vis India in any future discussions of its differences with China. For India it also meant that with the erosion of a buffer state its northern region stood exposed to the threats of a state, the expansive ambitions of which were too obvious to be missed by any discerning diplomat. India may have been quite generous in giving up all the inherited privileges which in the

changed conditions looked somewhat irrelevant but as a *Quid pro quo* it should have firmly stood for the Tibetan autonomy which it had intermittently enjoyed for the past several hundred years. India's stance on this issue not only caused the demise of a system which had served as a bulwark to our country's security but completely transformed the balance of power in South and Southeast Asia.

However, after the basic agreement was signed, detailed trade talks began in Delhi. As a result, on 14 October 1954, a trade pact was signed and notes exchanged between the two countries. The trade agreement gave China two more important concession; first, provision of reasonable facilities for entry into the port of Calcutta and subsequent movement to the Tibetan region of such commercial goods as could not be obtained in India; second, establishment of a branch of the People's Bank of China in Calcutta. The first concession allowed the Chinese to transport to Tibet a large volume of goods required for the maintenance of troops there though these could not be included in the category of military supplies. The Chinese troops in Tibet were always maintained only by the supplies that reached them from India and Nepal. Even during 1957-58 when the Chinese troops were suppressing the people of Tibet supplies were made from India.

According to Prince Paul of Greece who was then considered an authority on Tibetan affairs, the Indian authorities in the late 1950s, in a way, assisted the Chinese in getting over Tibet. The *London Times* quoted him as saying that 'the Chinese armies were receiving supplies along the only road from the Indian border to Lhasa'. 'I discovered myself that truck convoys, alleged by India to be loaded with rice, were full of military supplies' he observed.[37] With the help of these arms, the Chinese captured Tibet. The external affairs ministry took the view that for a landlocked area like Tibet, transport facilities across a neighbouring country like India were permissible under international law.

The other facility of establishing a Chinese bank in Calcutta was mainly meant for the Chinese residents there. The fear was that it could keep many of their transactions secret. The government did not seek in return any such facility in China partly because there were hardly any Indian nationals in China to claim

such facility and partly because the Chinese in keeping with the financial policy of their country were not going to make use of an Indian bank for their transactions. Indian official view was that it was one of the normal facilities given to any country having diplomatic relations and that we did not ask for our own bank in China made no difference.

India had given up its extra territorial rights in Tibet acquired by the former British rulers on the ground that they had been extorted from a weak Tibet by the powerful imperial powers in 1904 and later extended in 1914. But the renunciation of these rights was done not in favour of a weak and friendly Tibet but in favour of a strong and belligerent China which had captured and enslaved Tibet.

The truth of the matter was that even if we wanted to retain these rights we could not do so. After all, force is the ultimate sanction to secure one's claim. In military power, India was not a match to China even to protect our rights. We could not resist their evicting our military guards or their taking over our official installations if we had not agreed to part with them. If they had ordered us to close our trade agencies or the consulate as they had done earlier in Kashgar we would have to acquiesce. We could have disallowed the Chinese to open a consulate in Bombay, a bank in Calcutta or trade agencies in Kalimpong and Calcutta, but all this would have resulted in the presence of a hostile, powerful China along the 2000 mile northern frontier with possibilities of all sorts of mischief that it could create there. There was no alternative left for the government but to adopt a friendly approach. But never had there been an example in history of appeasement ever satisfying an aggressor. This we learnt later at a considerable cost. Meanwhile, we could say with shame that we could not save Tibet, but at least we could save our skin.

6

DALAI LAMA ENTERS INDIA

In November 1956, the Mahabodh Society invited Dalai Lama to visit India to take part in the ceremonies commemorating the 2500th anniversary of the enlightenment of Buddha. For months, the Chinese would not allow him to leave Lhasa and instead suggested that a representative be sent. As it was likely to cause concern in all Buddhist countries, China reluctantly agreed but subject to the condition that Panchen Lama would accompany him. Since Panchen Lama was in the good books of the Chinese, he was expected to keep an eye on Dalai Lama's activities. Incidentally Chou En-lai was also in India on a return visit which in his view, would be a good opportunity to overawe Dalai. In this context it should also be mentioned that in the preceding year, Dalai had been to China where he stayed for over six months during which time, the Chinese hoped, that he would be 'brainwashed' and given a new ideological orientation.

Dalai Lama visited all the important pilgrim places associated with the name of Buddha and thoroughly enjoyed his trips. Meanwhile, during Dalai's absence, the Chinese started a drive to introduce the socalled reforms during the process of which they were very highhanded towards those who opposed them. Dalai Lama felt much distressed and apprehended that on his return he might have to face a worse situation. So he expressed his unwillingness to return to Tibet. This message he sought to convey

to the Prime Minister. Nehru advised him to return as his presence among the people would keep them in high spirits otherwise they would get demoralized and fell irretrievably under Chinese domination. He assured him to have talks with Chou En-lai in this connection. This he did and told the Chinese Prime Minister about the rigours of the Chinese presence in Tibet. Chou admitted that the local officers might have committed excesses and assured that he would speak to Mao not to accelerate the process of communism in Tibet. This made Dalai Lama change his mind. On 1 April 1957 he returned to Lhasa which he had left on 20 November 1956.

REVOLT IN LHASA

On his return Dalai Lama found the situation very disturbing. Even the Chinese were reported to have sent messages to him whilst in India to hurry back to Tibet to help them restore peace by his presence. The main cause of worry was that despite the most ruthless steps taken by the Chinese, the Khampa rebellion in East Tibet was still raging. The main cause of the revolt in Tibet was due to the large settlement of the Chinese in their region. Even the appeal issued by the Dalai to maintain peace had hardly any impact as it was a very sensitive issue. In the midst of such a war like situation, thousands of people migrated towards Lhasa causing serious problem of shelter and food; it had also become difficult to maintain civic services. In keeping with the assurances of Chou En-lai some forces were withdrawn and officially it was announced that no reforms would be introduced in Tibet for at least five years.

While in India Dalai Lama, in consultation with Chou En-lai had invited Nehru to visit Tibet; Nehru had accepted their invitation. Dalai was under the impression that during Nehru's visit Chou would also be there and this would give him an opportunity to discuss some problems which were confronting all the three leaders. But in July 1958, the Chinese withdrew their consent on the plea that it would not be safe for Nehru to be in Tibet in those troubled times. To the Chinese it would have been some sort of mediation which they did not want as Tibet was to them a domestic issue. Tibetans were sorely disappointed. Nehru later, while visiting Bhutan had gone right up to the borders but the Tibetans were not allowed even to meet him.

By the middle of 1958, the Chinese had completed their hold on all parts of Tibet and the arterial road from South China to Sinkiang was ready and even radial roads had been completed to the borders of India, Nepal, Bhutan and Sikkim. By the beginning of 1959 they had realized that the Khampa rebellion would require a strong hand and accordingly by the end of February 1959 nearly two hundred thousand troops had been massed.

In the meanwhile, a news became current that the Dalai Lama was invited for a theatrical show in the military complex. Dalai Lama put it off till after the conclusion of the annual Monlan festival and his own religious examination. When these were over, the invitation was renewed and the Dalai Lama was reported to have agreed to attend the function on 10 March. But on 9 March, the Chinese sent for the chief of Dalai Lama's bodyguards and made a condition that the Dalai would have to come alone and that no Tibetan troops would cross the stone bridge which marked the boundary of the military camp. It was a strange condition which caused much suspicion. A few days earlier the Dalai was advised by Ngapo Shepe who was living in Chinese complex to seek shelter in the Chinese military camp. But he refused to do so. This time it was planned to lure the Dalai Lama into the Chinese military complex, isolate him from the rebels and fly him over to Peking declaring that he had gone over there of his own accord.[38] The idea of inviting him to a theatrical performance was a mere hoax.

This caused apprehension among the Tibetan leaders; over 10,000 people collected around the palace of Dalai Lama and demonstrated against the ruthlessly repressive policy of China. Three cabinet ministers were sent to explain the situation to the Chinese military chief. The ministers were harshly treated and held responsible for keeping Dalai Lama as their captive. The situation was getting worse and tension went on mounting. On 16 March, two explosions took place near the palace of Dalai Lama which were regarded as a precursor to heavy bombing by Chinese planes. On 17 March along with a few family members and trusted colleagues Dalai Lama left in disguise; the whole operation was carried out with utmost care and secrecy. He wanted to set up a government at Chuntze Dzong but finding it vulnerable he shifted to India.

On 31 March 1959, Dalai Lama crossed into India. He was received in accordance with the instructions from New Delhi by the political officer of Tawang subdivision of the NEFA. On 5 April Nehru said at a press conference that Dalai Lama was not expected to function politically in India. 'But' he added 'as the Dalai was greatly revered in India it is not our intention to put what might be called undesirable curbs on him'. Nehru realized the mood of the people and felt that Tibet was deeply rooted in national sentiment overriding party considerations.

In his first statement at Tezpur, Dalai Lama said that he had left Lhasa voluntarily, under no body's pressure. He also disclosed that the letters that he had written between 10 and 15 March to the Chinese military chief in Lhasa was to gain time and keep the Chinese in a state of suspense. He was given political asylum and shifted to a hill station in UP, Mussorie. In Rajya Sabha, on 4 May 1959 Nehru said that so far as the grant of political asylum to Dalai Lama was concerned, as a sovereign country India had every right to do so and nobody could be judge of that excepting Indian people. This was also justified from India's own security point of view, particularly the security of its northern frontier region where the population was predominantly Buddhist, though they were not Tibetans. Being happy with India's gesture they would help in maintaining peace on our border.

When Dalai Lama first arrived here, the government placed some restrictions on his political activities. But these restrictions were loosened when war broke out in October 1962. In the wake of war there had been several appeals from various political quarters to the government of India to give recognition to the Tibetan government in exile and the inclusion of escapee Tibetan military men in the Indian army. The government of India did not like the idea. Speaking in Parliament on 10 December 1963, Nehru reaffirmed the government's determination not to allow an 'emigre government' in India because, he said, 'it could mean India's undertaking to free the whole of Tibet, it is a large undertaking' for which India was not prepared. Despite such a categorical statement of the government, the Chinese continued to accuse the Indian government of setting up offices to employ and train the Tibetan guerrillas in exile in India to carry out armed subversive activities in Tibet.

Another event which caused tension between India and China was that on 10 March 1963, Dalai Lama proclaimed a new constitution for Tibet. The Chinese government came forward with a statement that the 'emigre government' was functioning under the wings of the Indian government. It did not conform to international law since India continued to maintain its diplomatic relations with China. The Chinese media saw in it the design of the US imperialists and Indian expansionists to seize the Chinese territory of Tibet by giving it an independent status. The Chinese seemed to have forgotten the elementary fact that the Tibetans domiciled in India had an inalienable right to express their reactions to the developments that were being introduced by the Chinese in Tibet and what they would plan to do if given a chance to return to their homeland. This was exactly what the Tibetans collectively had done in formulating their views on political, economic and social issues in the form of a constitution.

After the Indian government had lifted restrictions on the activities of the Dalai Lama the Chinese became very vociferous in criticising India for even the most innocuous activities which the Dalai was called upon to perform. The communications addressed to the Indian government were worded in a very offensive language. This caused much bitterness on personal level. In 1967, Dalai Lama was invited by a Japanese Buddhist society to visit Tokyo. There he remained exclusively busy in performing various religious ceremonies but the Chinese media accused him of making objectionable statements. This led to tension between China and Japan concerning their trade relations and the expulsion of the *Yomiuri Shimban* correspondent in Peking. The retaliation on the part of Peking against the Dalai Lama's visit to Japan seemed to indicate that the Chinese communists were still afraid of his influence on the Buddhists in Tibet and other countries. Likewise, whenever the domiciled Tibetans staged a protest demonstration at the Chinese embassy in Delhi, the Chinese media made a hue and cry implicating Indian government in the display of Tibetan resentment expressed in a peaceful way against the Chinese policies being followed in Tibet. This is because China was a stranger to the working of a democratic system of government in which people are entitled to basic human rights, one of them being freedom of speech and demonstration.

7

BORDER PROBLEM

The Chinese maps published in 1950 soon after the establishment of the People's Republic of China showed its boundary with India right up to the Brahmputra foothills. In reply to India's protest in February 1951, Chinese assured the government of India that those were old maps prepared during the Chiang Kai-shek regime. During his visit to China in October 1954, Nehru again brought to the notice of the Chinese government that he had seen some recent Chinese maps in which boundary between India and China was wrongly delineated.

China sought to set at rest Nehru's doubts by repeating the earlier explanation that they were merely a reproduction of old KMT maps which the new government had no time to revise. During his India visit in the winter of 1956 Chou was reported to have agreed that while there was no dispute regarding the border between the two countries, there were some petty problems which should be settled amicably by the representatives of the two governments. Chou was also said to have assured Nehru that as in the case of Burma, the government of China had accepted the boundary defined in 1914 by what is popularly known as Mc Mahon line he would recognize the same line marking the India-China border in the east but he would consult Tibetan authorities in this regard.

On 23 January 1959, Chou wrote to Nehru admitting that it

was true that the border question was not raised in 1954 when negotiations were being held between the representatives of the two countries for the agreement on trade and intercourse between Tibeten region of China and India. This was because the conditions were not yet ripe for its settlement. It was indeed a very intriguing statement. By 1959 the Chinese had consolidated their positions in Tibet, the Tibetan resistance had been shattered, the Chinese forces had considerably been reinforced and thousands of Chinese had been brought and settled along the Tibetan border lands. This is by what Chou meant when he referred to 'the situation being not ripe' for holding border talks with India. However, Chou suggested that till the boundary between the two countries was settled by mutual consultation, the two sides would maintain the status quo.

The Chinese started constructing a highway through Aksai Chin, which India claimed to be its territory, to provide a strategic link between Sinkiang and Tibet. The Indian military attache in Peking reported the matter to the government but the then ambassador R.K. Nehru did not like to forward it lest the Prime Minister disapproved it. A copy of it was sent to the defence ministry where this development was viewed with much concern. To celebrate the completion of this event at the end of 1957, the Chinese held a ceremony to which the Indian envoy as well as his military attache were invited though neither of them turned up. This was clearly meant to let the government of India know what the Chinese had done in their 'own territory' probably to forestall any attempt by India to question the propriety of their action.

For reasons to keep the matter confined to discussions between the two governments, the Indian authorities made no statement on this issue for public information though the press frequently published reports about it. Later on 28 August 1959, Nehru under pressure from several opposition leaders made a statement in the Parliament giving a brief report about the Chinese intervention in Ladakh with particular reference to the road built across Indian territory. But he was quick to add that these areas were extraordinarily remote, almost inaccessible and even if they tried to approach it, it took weeks and weeks to get there. He also referred to the vagueness in actual demarcation on the ground which made it difficult to know where the immediate border was although broadly it may be known. He assured that the matter

was under consideration and the data was being verified by both the Indian and Chinese sides.

In a statement in the Rajya Sabha three days later, Nehru specifically said that the Sinkiang-Tibet highway was completed in September 1957. The following year two reconnaissance parties were sent to the Aksai Chin area to find out the object of the recently built road and to check up whether it intruded into Indian territory. One of the parties was captured by the Chinese and later released. The other party returned and reported that the road passed through Indian territory. The Chinese note dated 1 November 1958 notified the release of the party and claimed that the road ran through Chinese territory. India in a rejoinder on 8 November countered the Chinese claim and this communication remained unanswered despite repeated reminders.[39] The confusion arose out of the fact that the boundary of the Aksai Chin region with China-Tibet had not been marked on the ground and once and twice questions had been raised about the exact alignment of this boundary. Old Chinese maps had shown a different alignment which supported their claim. In 1959, the Chinese built another highway west to the Aksai Chin road besides new feeder roads designed to supply their outposts.

In view of the deterioration in relations between the two countries Nehru wrote to Chou on 8 February to visit India and have talks with Indian leaders. He arrived here on 16 April 1960 and stayed for six days during which period he had detailed talks with several Indian leaders including G.B. Pant, home minister and Morarji Desai, finance minister. Morarji Desai, in his talks with Chou En-lai was quite frank in telling the Chinese leader that when nobody supported China, India took several steps in befriending them. For instance, India accepted their sovereignty over Tibet for which there was much domestic criticism of Nehru government. But China did not accept the condition of respecting autonomy of Tibet which, on the other hand, was completely obliterated by the policy of ruthless suppression followed by China in their attempt to 'modernise' Tibet. The flight of Dalai Lama to seek security in India was an eyesore to the entire civilised world. India signed with China the concept of Panchsheel enunciating five noble principles of peaceful coexistence, but they were honoured more in breach than observance. The result was that all

social, economic and religious contacts between the people of the two countries were completely snapped. India did not raise any dispute about the boundaries but for extraneous reasons China started provoking India by repeated incursions. It was too much for Chou to stomach all this plain speaking.

However, it was reported that during the talks Chou proposed a sort of barter deal according to which China was prepared to accommodate India along the NEFA frontier by staying behind the Mc Mohan line if India would be willing to accommodate China in Ladakh by accepting the line of actual control in that region. The proposal of Chou underlined the vital importance China attached to the highway they had constructed through Aksai Chin. But there was a serious snag in this proposal. Chou was referring to the actual line as it existed in 1960 by which time China had occupied a good deal of Indian territory. The talk of actual line started in 1956 when the Chinese had a small land of Indian territory on the western side of Aksai Chin in their occupation but since then the Chinese had been surreptitiously occupying more and more land to keep India away as far as possible from the Aksai Chin region. By 1959 they began talking of a new actual line. Nehru or for that matter any one in his place would never have accepted the proposal of a ever changing line of actual control. Finally, it was announced that the talks could end in no agreement on the vexed question of border demarcation between the two countries. To give respectability to the fruitless negotiations it was agreed that the officials of the two governments would meet to examine all relevant documents in support of the stands of the two governments and report.

The officials of the two governments met at Peking, Delhi and Rangoon and submitted their reports as directed. The government of India published its version on 14 February 1961 while the Chinese government took a year to make it public in April 1962. On an objective analysis Indian report was more comprehensive than that of the Chinese based as it was on the evidence of tradition, custom and usage. It proved that the boundary alignment shown by India was the long established one in support of which treaties, agreements and diplomatic exchanges were cited. The Chinese side produced only a few vague and imprecise documents of recent dates which were inconsistent with their claim and arguments

and contradictory in facts. Several items of evidence cited by them were found to prove the Indian case. The alignments claimed by the Chinese were not supported by the maps that they had placed before the negotiating parties. For example, the alignments shown in the Chinese maps officially given at the talks in 1960 were altogether different in the Ladakh area from the alignments shown in the 1956 map which was endorsed by Chou En-lai in December 1959. The new alignments covered some 2000 sq. miles more of Indian territory.[40]

FORWARD POLICY

With the April 1960 summit between Nehru and Chou En-lai being a failure India's China policy had reached a cul-de-sac. The Chinese forces, called 'frontier guards', had advanced into Indian territory and established several posts in what they claimed to be their territory but which in fact was the Indian territory. The use of force to eject the Chinese from what was our land would mean a war for which India was not prepared. On the other hand acquiescence to the status quo on the border was ruled out as it would amount to acceptance of the Chinese ownership over our land. A third way out of the impasse was reported to be that New Delhi should assert its right by despatching properly equipped patrols into the area which was occupied by the Chinese, since any prolonged failure to do so would imply a tacit acceptance of Chinese occupation and a surrender to Peking's threat to cross the Mc Mahon line should Indian patrols penetrated into the disputed area of Ladakh.[41] This line of action came to be known as the 'forward policy' of India. It was not formulated in the normal process of government making policy decisions. It emerged out of the situation in which the government found itself at the beginning of 1960.

It appeared to the government in November 1959 that unless all the vacant spaces on our side of the frontier were occupied by Indian troops or police, there was every danger of the Chinese surreptitiously occupying all the rest of the area.[42] Accordingly Nehru instructed the officials concerned to see that all the gaps were filled by moving forward Indian troops to the farthest point of our border. Nearly 43 Indian posts were set up between 1959 and 1962. The move, though confined within our own territory, caused annoyance among the Chinese as their claim was that India

was trying to encroach on their side of the territory. In the first flush of war, all the 43 Indian posts were demolished by the Chinese on the plea that what they had done was within their own territory.

The objective of the forward policy was first to block the potential lines of further Chinese advance and secondly to establish Indian presence in Aksai Chin which would make Indian participation in the joint withdrawal proposed by Nehru more than theoretical and thus give strength to the diplomatic lever for getting the Chinese out of the area. It was also the intention to undermine tenuous control of the disputed area by the interposition of Indian posts between the Chinese positions thus cutting their supply lines and ultimately forcing them to withdraw. Another illusion from which the policy-makers in Delhi suffered was that China would not go to war against India unless India attacked any of the Chinese posts. Chinese had repeatedly warned that the assertion of Indian claims in the western sector would follow retaliation across the Mc Mahon line.

The government had to adopt this policy because there was too much pressure from all opposition parties and there was silent sympathy from the Congress side also. It was denied that any such action would amount to war as 'to defend your own territory was not to wage war; it would be a police action on your own territory; it was to throw the bandits out from your territory; it would be consistent with the policy of Indian government'. This is how the opposition parties argued their case. The parties seemed to be insistent in their pressure on the government probably because the general elections were round the corner. While Chou was in Delhi a mass demonstration was staged in front of Nehru's residence demanding that the government would not yield to the pressure of Chou En-lai's presence in Delhi. Nehru came out and assured the crowd that not an inch of Indian soil would be yielded to China. Chou, on his part, left Delhi very embittered and determined to teach India a lesson.

Before he left, Chou gave a press conference at which he made a six-point proposal which was described as 'six-points of proximity' between the two sides. These in his view, would lead to a mutually acceptable solution. They were: (1) there is a dispute regarding the boundary between the two countries; (2) there is a line of actual control up to which each side is exercising

administrative jurisdiction; (3) in determining the boundary question between the two countries certain geographical principles such as watersheds, river valleys and mountain passes should be equally applicable to all sectors of the boundary; (4) a settlement of the boundary question between the two countries should take into account the national feelings of the two peoples towards the Himalaya and the Karakoram mountains; (5) pending a settlement of the boundary question between the two countries both sides should keep to the line of actual control; one should not put forward territorial claims as pre-condition but individual adjustments may be made; (6) In order to ensure tranquility on the border, both sides should continue to refrain from patrolling along all sectors of the boundary.[43]

The Indian approach was different; it continued to maintain that there had never been any doubt as to where exactly Tibet boundary with India lay till China violated that boundary giving rise to a dispute which had never been there. All that was necessary was for China to go back to the position obtaining before China disturbed it. The Indian team of officials made this point clear at their meeting with their Chinese counterparts at Rangoon in December 1960. It was summarized under five following heads: (1) there has been a traditional and customary boundary between India and Tibet; (2) China had never questioned the boundary and in fact accepted and acquiesced in what India had always taken to be their traditional and customary alignment; (3) the Sino-Indian boundary has always been delimited either formally or through a historical process; (4) India had traditionally exercised administrative control up to the boundary and China should desist from disturbing the status quo as it had been in 1959; (5) marginal adjustments for rectification of the boundary could be made by mutual agreement if found necessary after consultation.[44]

EXPIRY OF THE 1954 AGREEMENT

On 31 December 1961, China in a note reminded India that the 1954 agreement was due to expire in six months and proposed negotiations for a new one to replace it. It was when the situation on the border was very tense that Peking made a mention of it probably holding that under the pressure of Chinese violation of Indian border, New Delhi would agree to the extension of the

agreement. It was an opportune moment for China to have referred this proposal to India. But India was not prepared to act under such a pressure. In the first instance, it was essential that China should itself reverse its aggressive policies to restore a climate in which such a subject be discussed. China saw no reason to link this subject with the wider issue of boundary question.

India declined to negotiate a new agreement in view of what had happened in Tibet giving rise to a near-war situation on the border. The trade which the 1954 agreement had meant to promote never made any headway because of the deteriorating relations between the two countries. Its continuation would have implied that the five principles of peaceful co-existence had been faithfully observed which was not the case. Moreover, during the process of its working China had imposed arbitrary regulations on Indian nationals in clear violation of not only the preamble of the agreement but also its detailed provisions.

The Sino-Indian agreement of 1954 lay in shreds by the time when proposal was made for its renewal. Even the government admitted that the provisions of the treaty were not observed. The Chinese began a systematic harassment of our Lhasa consulates and trade agency staff. Indian traders continued to suffer difficulties because of the facilities to repatriate their legitimate profits being denied after the Indian and Tibetan currencies were declared as illegal tenders. The result was that pilgrimages of Tibetans to the holy places of Buddhism ceased and the oppression of Indian pilgrims visiting Kailash and Mansarover increased. There was the typical case of Brahmchari Atma Chaitnya who, when on his way to Kailash was searched and harried and compelled to sign a confession that the homeopathic medicines he was carrying were intended to poison the local people. All this was meant to convert Tibet into a forbidden land.[45]

The agreement lapsed on 3 June 1962; India withdrew its trade agents from Yatung and Gyantse in Tibet; China withdrew its personnel from Kalimpong and Calcutta. The consul general at Lhasa was maintained for another six months until India decided to inform the closure of consular missions in both countries from 15 December. Thus ended the agencies that were created under the 1954 agreement to facilitate contacts between India and Tibet in the context of new relationship created by its takeover by China.

PRECURSORS TO ATTACK

The government of India did not set up any border outpost right along the traditional frontier. This was because the area was inhabited very sparsely and they had no reason to anticipate any aggressive intention on the part of the Chinese authorities. The government activities remained confined to sending periodic police patrol parties in that region. The same claim was made by China that the frontier guards of the peoples liberation army had all along been patrolling the entire area. Indian reconnaissance parties were sent in Ladhakh area in 1954, '55 and 56' and they found no evidence of the Chinese occupation. For the first time in 1957 signs of intrusion were witnessed in the region.

An Indian patrol party in this region was detained by the Chinese in the summer of 1958 and in reply to the protest the Chinese referred to their frontier guards having detained the Indian party because they were in Chinese territory. The next year the Chinese armed forces further intruded in Ladakh region and arrested another Indian patrol party. In October 1959 the Chinese further penetrated in Ladakh, killed nine Indian guards and ten others were taken in custody. China had thus by 1959 already begun to resort to force to occupy what it claimed to be its territory.

In June and September 1960 the Chinese forced their way into Taktsang Gompo in eastern sector and northern part of Sikkim. In October they came up to Hot Spring in Ladakh; in August 1961, they established three new checkposts in Ladakh and constructed roads linking these posts with rear bases. Early in 1962 they conducted aggressive forward patrolling in the western sector and warned India against the presence of Indian troops in that region.

In a bid to resolve the question Indian government in the letter dated 14 May 1962 repeated what Nehru had suggested to Chou in November 1959. He had told the Chinese Premier that to maintain peace on the border Indian troops would be withdrawn in the western sector to the west of the line shown in the Chinese maps of 1956 and the Chinese should withdraw to the east of the boundary shown in Indian maps. This would apply to the armed men as well as unarmed civilian and administrative personnel so that the entire area claimed by both sides would become no-man's-

land. This was going to be interim arrangement which included India's willingness to accede to China's claim for Aksai Chin for the time being.[46] The Chinese in their reply dated 2 June 1962 rejected India's proposal on the plea that it was a negative reply and also because that it would not accept India's suggestion that the road in Aksai Chin would also be subject to further negotiations. To them it was the Chinese territory which was not negotiable.

The Chinese government rejected this offer and went on setting up new posts. The Chinese troops also stepped up their forward patrolling practice in the western sector leading to the encirclement of an Indian post in the Galwan valley and also other small checkposts in the region. On 26 July the government of India sought the cooperation of the Chinese authorities to stop these intrusions so that the negotiations between the two governments may begin to end this impasse. While diplomatic notes were being exchanged, the Chinese troops suddenly on 8 September 1962 marched across the well established and till then peaceful boundary in the eastern sector, viz., the Mc Mahon line. All these border incidents seemed to be a prelude to a massive onslaught which was soon to be launched. Meanwhile, Peking issued new maps to support their encroachment and initiate new territorial claims.

On psychological plane, the Chinese were preparing their people to be ready to face an eventuality in which they would find themselves face to face with Indian belligerents. In a document circulated to its embassies abroad in 1961, the Chinese government laid down the following lines of political strategy: (1) friendly relations with small Asian countries be strengthened, border treaties be concluded and the problem of overseas Chinese be settled; special consideration be given to develop relations with Pakistan and efforts be made to conclude border settlement with it; (2) anti-Chinese activities of reactionary Indian leadership be faced vigorously and India be forced to adopt a defensive attitude on the border; (3) after the Ladakh incident in which 9 Indian constables were killed in October 1959, a wave of anti-Chinese campaign spread over the entire country. China countered it by retaining the initiative on the border, e.g., by suggesting a 20 km, non-militarized belt on both sides of the line of actual control and also by the visit of Chou En-lai to India to carry on negotiations

with Nehru; (4) the Chinese would unite with all forces which were available and would deal with American imperialism as the main enemy. With this broad framework the country against which the Chinese would have to struggle chiefly was India. It is obvious from the document that the Chinese were prepared with a strategy which they had to adopt in facing India in an armed conflict.[47]

8

CHINESE ATTACK

At exactly five in the morning on 20 October 1962, Chinese launched a massive attack on India with an army of twenty thousand troops. It was no incident or a border conflict but a full scale and obviously well planned attack launched skilfully across the world's highest mountain range. The Chinese also struck in Ladakh at the other end of the frontier. Eleven posts in the western sector and five in the eastern sector were attacked, some were taken by the Chinese, the others were abandoned within three hours of the fighting. This was the end of year of negligence, months of miscalculation and weeks of indecision. India had an army of four lakhs but due to our stubborn refusal to think in strategic terms only 6000 men were employed in the battle against a much powerful enemy. This flimsy barrier was pierced with consummate ease by the powerful force which the Chinese had mustered to teach India a lasting lesson.[48] Our soldiers put up a spirited fight against overwhelming odds and rose to super human heights of chivalry. They were short of rations for which they did not care and even when their ammunition was getting exhausted they fought to the last bullet. In three short hours the flowers of two regular battalions gave their life at the call of duty. The Chinese later admitted that they had suffered the maximum casualties of the NEFA fighting in the first battle.[49]

On 24 October, four days after the massive invasion of India, the Chinese put forward three point proposal to ceasefire; (1) both parties would respect the line of actual control as of 7 November

1959 along the entire Sino-Indian border and armed forces of each side withdraw twenty km from this line and disengage; (2) If India accepted this proposal, the Chinese troops in the eastern sector would withdraw to the north of the line of actual control, at the same time neither side would cross the traditional customary line in the middle and western sectors of the border; (3) talks be held between the Prime Ministers of the two countries at a time and place convenient to both.

In November 1959, in the western sector, the 'line of actual control' was no line really but a series of Chinese positions on Indian territory, established forcibly and unilaterally, altering the traditional boundary. The November 1959 line would join all the Chinese positions going up to Aksai Chin road which the Chinese had constructed in Indian territory. During the next three years, that is by September 1962, the Chinese constructed a number of military roads and posts. By 1962, this net work of military posts was at certain points more than a hundred miles to the west of the Chinese positions in 1959. The latest line of actual control not only envisaged the inclusion of all the Chinese posts established since 1959 but also the forty odd Indian posts which existed till the Chinese invasion on 20 October 1962.

The difference between the Chinese control line of November 1959 and the latest line was as much as 5000 to 6000 sq. miles. By the three point proposal the Chinese wanted India to withdraw yet another 20 km (12.5 miles) from the latest Chinese line inside territory accepted by the Chinese themselves as Indian. On the other hand the Chinese withdrawal of 20 km would be wholly inside the territory that India had claimed as its own and in which it had already set up 43 military posts. Acceptance of this proposal would mean India's tacit consent to China's claims to the territory which rightly belonged to India but which China had usurped. The net effect would be that the entire network of Chinese posts which existed on 20 October 1962, would remain intact while all Indian defence posts in Indian territory claimed by Chinese would be eliminated.

The Chinese alleged that the Indian government refused to restore the state of boundary of 7 November 1959 but insisted on what it was on 8 September 1962 when the undeclared war started.

This was obviously because since 1959, the Indian government had seized by force large tract of Chinese territory in which they had set up 43 defence posts. The fact of the matter was that as on 7 November 1959, the Chinese had by no means attained a consolidated line in Ladakh but had established only a few scattered posts on what India claimed to be its territory. These posts had been progressively established by intruding Chinese troops since 1957 by surreptitious means. By a process of gradual intrusion they occupied by September 1962 more than 6000 sq. miles of additional territory and later by their massive aggression on 20 October, further 2500 sq. miles went under Chinese control, till they finally reached the line which later they claimed was the line of actual control in November 1959. In fact, when the Chinese referred to the line of actual control as on 7 November 1959, from which they proposed to carry out withdrawals in both eastern and western sectors it was the line up to which the Chinese forces had reached first as a result of their intrusion and later by the massive aggression mounted after 20 October 1962.

Nehru in his message of 26 October 1962 addressed to the heads of Afro-Asian states said: 'this is not a mere boundary dispute or a question of small territorial frontier adjustment. Apart from the vast and fantastic claims that China had made, China had already occupied 12000 sq. miles of Indian territory during the last few years. While notes were being exchanged for arranging talks and discussion to ease tension and even dates and places were being suggested further aggression by China started on 8 September 1962 and more areas of Indian territory were occupied in a new sector. He then referred to the Chinese massive attack which started on 20 October resulting in serious conflict and bringing matters to a crisis. The issue involved was not one of small territorial gains one way or the other but of standards of international behaviour between the neighbouring countries. India would continue to resist aggression both to preserve her honour and integrity and to prevent international standards from deterioration into the law of jungle which was 'might is right'. He warned the international community that the crisis was not only of India but of the world and it would have far reaching consequences on the standards of international behaviour. Finally, he hoped 'in this hour of crisis when we are engaged in resisting the aggression, we are confident that we still have the sympathy and support of all countries not

only because of their friendly relations with us but also because our struggle is in the interest of world peace and is directed to the elimination of deceit, duplicity and force in international relations'.

The second Chinese offensive began on 15 November, the day after the three point proposal had been rejected by India. This time the Chinese troops attacked on a 500 mile front both in NEFA and in the Western sector where they seemed to have not reached their targets. India was no more equipped to meet the attack in either sector and soon the debacle was a shocking spectacle. The rapidity with which the Chinese forces marched into Indian territory was frightening. Its enormity was realised when it was noted that China had succeeded in occupying an area in India equal in size of England. In eastern sector they came right down up to the Brahmputra valley in Assam capturing all the checkposts that Indian army had set up. In Ladakh also, the Chinese made a clean sweep of the area that India claimed to be its own and as a symbolic gesture a few army posts had been set up. Peking took advantage of this situation and suddenly announced that from midnight on 22 November, the Chinese forces would ceasefire along the entire Sino-Indian border and as from 1 December they would start going back to positions 20 km behind the line of actual control which existed on 7 November 1959.

The ceasefire declaration threatened India with resumption of hostilities if Indian forces would advance to the Mc Mahon line or occupy the Thagla and Longju areas in eastern sector, if in the middle sector Indian forces would fail to withdraw 20 km or continue to administer Barahoti and if in the western sector Indian forces would fail to withdraw 20 km or if they would attempt to reoccupy 43 defensive posts overrun by the Chinese during the latest aggression.[50]

China had won the war before it was fought. India was overwhelmed. It became clear that it was not a practical proposition to defend India without using the military might of America. On 19 November 1962, Nehru sent to Kennedy urgent request for help and the communication was delivered by Indian envoy B.K. Nehru the same night. This was not a request in general terms but a specific appeal for air protection. Even the number of operational air squadrons was mentioned presumably in

consultation with the service chiefs of Indian army. Nehru had asked for 16 squadrons of fighting aircrafts manned by American personnel. Kennedy responded immediately. He also ordered the U.S. sixth fleet in the Mediterranean and the US seventh fleet in the Pacific to proceed towards Bay of Bengal. Perhaps a carrier or two were also set on the move as a warning to China.

Americans knew how to give a signal to an aggressor. It was a signal that if the Chinese advanced any more they would be doing so at their own risk. The signal was reported to have been gone through not directly by Wshington but through a powerful medium, the government of USSR. It should be recalled that there was an interval of two days between Nehru's message to Kennedy and China's 'unilateral' declaration of ceasefire.[51]

As regards the casualties suffered by the Indian army, the defence ministry released the following figures: killed 1383, missing 1696, captured 3968, the total came to 7043. Twenty-six of the Indians died of wounds in captivity, the rest were repatriated. About ninety per cent of the Indian casualties were suffered in NEFA. Not one Chinese prisoner was taken by the Indians, who did not want to add to their liabilities of restricted rations and other material supplies. Where the Indian troops stood and fought, the Chinese suffered heavy casualties. At Thembang, for example, where the Chinese had concentrated their forces on 17 November to face Indian troops, the Chinese suffered between three to four thousand casualties.[52]

WHY CEASEFIRE?

The Chinese had come down to the foothills and plains and they were faced with supply problems. The Chinese troops came equipped with supplies to last them a few weeks, they retreated when their supplies got exhausted. They obviously did not want to waste their limited supplies of oil and other commodities to hold on to NEFA. With the advent of winter all the hills of the region would be snow-bound which would create an insurmountable problem of the logistics. Chinese lines of communication which had already been extended to a great extent creating a problem of supplying urgently needed commodities to the troops on the war front, were likely to be choked by the snow.

The Anglo-American offer of immediate military aid was yet another intimidating factor. Every day from 3 November, eight air ship-load of American arms supplies started landing at Calcutta airport. This was a clear warning to China to desist from taking any further step. Earlier President Kennedy had announced that he would help India to maintain herself against an attack if such an attack should come again. Not content with generalisation, Kennedy gave an immutable warning to China: 'if China advanced any further, they would be forcing the hands of the President of the US to take adequate action'.[53] Moreover, the trends of world opinion were rising in censure against the Chinese aggression on India. Unfriendly reactions were more widespread than Peking had calculated endangering China's profession of being a peaceful nation. As many as 75 countries had given their moral support to India.

What worried China most was the attitude of the Soviet Union. Russia was so far pre-occupied with the Cuban crisis. During that period Mosow endorsed Peking's proposal and advised India to start talks with China. Later when facts came to the notice of Khrushchev he was furious at Mao Tse-tung for creating a crisis with an ally who stood with China on so many crucial issues. This amounted to an ultimatum which the Chinese could ignore at their own risk and this they had not the courage to do. The Soviet disapproval of Chinese action vis-a-vis India proved that the first major fissure in the Sino-Soviet relations had surfaced for all to see. Khrushchev was reported to have written to Nehru that India's obtaining arms aid from the USA to defend herself against China would not be misconstrued by the Soviet Union. India found more support from the communist countries who followed the example of Khrushchev. All these factors induced the Chinese to stop a dangerous adventure they had embarked upon before things began to go wrong for them.

The unilateral declaration of ceasefire was made under the compulsion of circumstances that seemed to go against China. It was not the victory of the Chinese performance as such but more of India's weakness that marked this tragic event. The defence minister Y.B. Chavan had to admit several inadequacies from which Indian army suffered. According to his own reading the Indian army was not trained to fight a war in hilly and forest areas of NEFA and snow clad Himalayas in the north western

sector. They were unaware of Chinese preparations which they had been making for the past two years. What was worse, the Indian troops did not have enough protective snow-clothings; for them it was an ordeal to face the war situation in the border region with inadequate provisions; our intelligence service was inadequate and most of the wireless sets and signals were old and too heavy for operation in mountain terrain. Chinese communications, on the other hand, were far more developed with roads much nearer the Chinese forward posts.[54]

A word about our lack of preparation. Our leaders lived in the world of their own make-believe; they never realistically attempted to study the dangers of Chinese threats. During the days of crisis Nehru was reported to have said that the Chinese were not really strong as they had their own troubles and internal dissensions due to food shortage and unpopular dictatorial regime. Besides, they had the problem of Tibet on their hand. The impact of such political statements from the Prime Minister himself that China would not attack India had seeped down to the senior staff level in the army also and to a great extent had affected India's military preparations. In 1961 when the Chinese threat was no longer a hypothetical question but merely a matter of time the government reluctantly took up some steps to improve our defensive potential. At that time, Nehru was reported as saying that any additional defence expenditure would cause a major economic setback. He was in favour of marshalling indigenous resources rather wasting valuable foreign exchange abroad. On another occasion when the government was asked to sanction some money for the army, Nehru said that there would be no war with China, all the scare the army high command was making was a military miscalculation.[55]

Every one familiar with the state of Indian politics then knew of the clash between Desai, finance minister and Menon, defence minister, a clash which resulted in the armed forces being starved of urgently needed funds. One of the main causes of our defeat was the chaotic state of affairs created by Krishna Menon in the defence ministry. He caused friction among the senior officers by patronising his favourites at the cost of those who were competent and efficient. In the name of indigenous production of war material he was more interested in getting gadgets of daily use, than in enhancing the quality of lethal weapons. He was one with Nehru

in believing that China would be the last to attack India. Quite curiously he was more apprehensive of Pakistan than China.

CHINESE REACTION

Chou addressed a letter on 15 November 1962 to the Afro-Asian leaders in which he repudiated India's viewpoint. He held that the border disputes among the liberated countries were rooted in the policy of former imperialist powers. In the context of the new developments such disputes should be solved in the light of the five principles of peaceful coexistence and the ten principles adopted at the Bandung conference. Reiterating the reasonable attitude China had adopted in these matters, Chou referred to the boundary agreement which his government had signed with Burma and Nepal. In his view, it was evidence of China's friendly spirit and genuineness in solving boundary question by peaceful means. He blamed India for resisting such magnanimity. He also blamed India for making an unilateral alteration in the Sino-Indian traditional and customary alignment in its official maps published in 1954. The Chinese contention was that the version of the Sino-Indian boundary insidiously contrived by British imperialism was accepted by India who, in turn, tried to impose this version on China as the delimited boundary between China and India.[56] Chou took special care to bring to the notice of Afro-Asian leaders that the Indian government had openly begged military aid from the US to boost its case. Thus the Nehru government had finally shed its cloak of policy of nonalignment. The more Nehru would depend on American aid the greater would be the pressure on him to oppose China; and the more he persisted in opposing China, the greater would be the need for him to depend on US imperialism.[57]

China, as a first step in its diplomatic war decided to isolate India from the other small neighbouring countries. It tried to cultivate Nepal with provisions of economic assistance, active participation in the scientific development projects and offers to train Nepalese civilians. The Chinese also decided to construct a road connecting Nepal with Tibet and signed a border agreement. These steps signified China's political and economic penetration into Nepal which was strategically very crucial to India. The same year the Chinese government rushed through a border agreement with Burma in which it was reported to have accepted Mc Mahon

line as a frontier between the two countries. To further its end to keep India isolated from her neighbours, Peking mooted a proposal for a Himalayan federation comprising Nepal, Bhutan, Sikkim, NEFA and Nagaland.

In November 1962, high Chinese officials addressing overseas Chinese declared, under instructions from the top leadership, that there would be a stalemate in the actual fighting until next summer and further developments would depend on foreign military aid to India because without such aid there was no chance of India standing alone against China. They were also assured that the positions held in Ladakh could not be abandoned; in the east the recognition of the Mc Mahon line would be resolutely resisted and it is China that would decide where the line lay. In the meantime efforts would continue to be made to condemn Nehru government and to isolate it from the Indian people through the leftist forces in India. Finally, China would continue to propagate that it did not mean any war, it wanted border dispute to be settled peacefully.[58]

Chinese refuted the western allegation that it was out to humble India to seize the Asian leadership or to put a brake on India's development by forcing her to build up militarily. The Chinese leaders never supposed that any country but China could ever aspire to be the leader of Asia. India particularly with its capitalist economy and national bourgeoisie government could never challenge China in a race of economic development. But some of the Indian leaders suffered from superiority complex by claiming to have established a stable democratic system admired all over the world for sustaining economic system which was much superior to China's. This sort of unrealistic thinking could be exposed only if it was demonstrated on the battlefield how fallacious were their assumptions.

There was another dimension in which the Chinese thinking worked. The Sino-Indian dispute had become a factor in causing ill-feeling between Moscow and Peking. A blow at India might bring what the Chinese saw as Nehru's covert alliance with the Americans against themselves into the open and so expose the ideological error of Moscow's support for India.[59] American commitment to India's side was clear and by striking a protege,

China would be flouting the patron. Thus China wanted to kill two birds with one stone, to humiliate America and embarrass Russia. Finally, such a step that China would take could not fail to damage the Nehru government domestically and so help the revolutionary forces to launch a left oriented mass movement. Peking dreamt of seeing the Chinese type of revolution repeated in India.

On the eve of the Colombo conference on 8 December, India received a sharply worded warning from China demanding a 'clear and definite' reply to three questions: does the Indian government agree or does it not agree to a ceasefire?, does the Indian government agree or does it not agree that the armed forces of the two sides should disengage and withdraw twenty km each from the 7 November 1959 line of actual control? and does the Indian government agree or does it not agree that officials of the two sides should meet and discuss matters relating to the twenty km withdrawal of the armed forcs of each country from the line of actual control of 7 November 1959 to form a demilitarized zone?

Indian government did not respond to this letter of threat but Nehru in a speech in the Parliament on the opening day of the Colombo conference, 10 December 1962, gave a point to point reply to China's three questions which he described as being 'couched in pre-emptory and dictatorial tone' and replete with factual distortions. First, India would do nothing to impede the implementation of the ceasefire declaration. Second, any negotiations would be possible only on the basis of undoing the further aggression committed by the government of China on Indian territory since 8 September 1962. Third, India did not agree to the socalled line of actual control of 7 November 1959 which was not in accordance with the facts.

In view of the sharp cleavage between the views of the two sides, there seemed to be no meeting ground, yet illustrating his willingness to explore all avenues to come to an understanding with China, Nehru suggested, with Parliamentary approval, that he would even be prepared to refer the basic dispute to the International Court of Justice, though this also would only come when aggression was vacated.[60] The House did not feel disposed to accept the proposal of Nehru despite his subsequent assura

that the government would take this step only when there was an opportune moment and the Parliament gave its approval.[61]

Later in a note dated 3 April 1963 the external affairs ministry suggested several constructive steps including international arbitration that could be taken to resolve the border problem in a peaceful manner. In a subsequent communication dated 1 May, Nehru again referred to it. Chou En-lai retorted that questions involving sovereignty of the states as the Sino-Indian boundary question did, could be settled only through direct negotiations between the two parties concerned and absolutely not through any form of arbitration. He repeated that the Chinese government had never agreed to refer the Sino-Indian boundary dispute to arbitration, nor would it ever do so. Nehru agreed that arbitration on the question of sovereignty was a concept that was unacceptable to India also but the Sino-Indian boundary dispute involved differences on interpretation of treaties, agreements, maps and the factual data relating to exercise of administration in the boundary areas under dispute. These differences were matters which were justiciable and capable of judicial interpretation either by the International Court of Justice at the Hague or by an arbitrator or arbitrators agreed upon between the two governments. Nehru agreed that in one of his earlier communications dated 7 August 1961 he did not consider that arbitration on the Sino-Indian dispute was called for because his people hoped that the differences between the two countries would be resolved by discussion and evaluation of the material advanced in support of their claims by both sides. But then the government of China tried to settle this dispute by force. It is in this context that the other peaceful method suggested by him, reference to the International Court of Justice or arbitration by impartial individuals agreed upon by both the countries had to be considered. There were a number of instances of such international arbitrations resorted to by various countries in the past.[62]

In closing his note Chou had the temerity to say that if the Indian government owing to internal and external requirements was not prepared to hold negotiations for the time being the Chinese government was willing to wait with patience.[63] Nehru took strong exception to this insinuation. He warned that the government of India had behind it the united support of the entire

people to the measures it had taken in the face of the aggressive and expansionist policies of the government of China. As regards the external pressure, the government of India ever since its independence had never been influenced in its decisions by any outside power. India had consistently pursued the policies that were guided by our desire to protect our national interest.

9

COLOMBO PROPOSALS

At the initiative of the Ceylon (Sri Lanka) government, the representatives of six Afro-Asian countries, Ceylon, Burma, Cambodia, Indonesia, United Arab Republic and Ghana met at Colombo from 10 to 12 December 1962 to consider the Sino-Indian border conflict and seek some compromise proposals which might bring the two countries to the conference table. They made it clear that it was not their intention to adjudicate on the dispute but to create the necessary climate for bilateral relations. In typical Chinese fashion, Chou En-lai sent a courteous telegram to the conference hoping that its efforts would promote negotiations between China and India to some successful result. Nehru speaking in the Parliament on 10 December expressed the hope that they would appreciate that there could be no compromise with aggression and the gains of aggression must be given up before both parties tried to resolve their dispute.[64]

As friends of both countries, the leaders of the six countries deliberately refrained from pronouncing the right or wrong of the Sino-Indian conflict nor did they brand China as aggressor. The proposals agreed to were not disclosed until they were formally published on 19 January 1963 well after Mrs. Bandarnaike, Prime Minister of Ceylon, had explained their contents both in Peking and New Delhi. The joint communique issued after the conference merely stated that members had reached unanimity regarding suggestions which they would convey to India and China in their attempt to bring those two countries together for negotiations to

consolidate the ceasefire and to settle the boundary dispute between them.

The proposals that emerged from their three-day discussions accepted by implication India's stand that talks could begin only if the territories occupied during the war were vacated by China. Ali Sabri, Prime Minister of UAR voiced these sentiments when he said at the opening session of the conference, that 'there must not be any territorial gain on account of military operations; this principle was in conformity with the spirit of Bandung conference'. However, in formulating the proposals, the participants held that neither side would derive benefit from military operations; stable ceasefire must precede any attempt at negotiations between China and India, any ceasefire arrangement must be without prejudice to the boundary claim of either party and prior to the establishment of ceasefire neither side should be requested to withdraw from territories which were admittedly theirs or from territory over which they exercised exclusive civilian administration.

In the light of these principles, the conference laid down the following proposals: (i) in the western sector the Chinese would carry out their twenty km. withdrawal of those military posts as had been proposed by the Chinese premier on 21 and 28 November 1962; (ii) the Indian government would keep their existing position reached as a result of the war; (iii) the areas vacated by the Chinese military withdrawal would be a demilitarized zone to be administered by civilian posts of both sides to be agreed upon without prejudice to the rights of the previous presence of both India and China in that area; (iv) in the eastern sector the line of actual control in the area recognized by both the governments would serve as a ceasefire line to their respective positions; remaining disputed areas would be settled in the future discussions between the two sides; (v) with regard to the problems of the middle sector they would be resolved by peaceful means without resorting to force.

The conference had mandated Mrs. Bandarnaike to convey the result of the deliberations to New Delhi and Peking but she preferred to go to Peking first as China's reaction to a great extent would determine India's stance on the issue. She told the Chinese leaders about what they were expected to do in compliance with

the proposals. But immediately before her arrival the Chinese reproduced a Chinese memorandum which was sent to India. It was to stress their point that they would consider the state of the border as it was on 7 November 1959 and not on 8 September 1962 as India had repeatedly suggested. India's date could not be a common baseline for separating the armed forces since at that time the positions of the two sides were interlocked in a jigsaw puzzle fashion. Moreover, Peking added that China was in effective jurisdiction over Aksai Chin area and Indian troops had only been able to establish positions on the Chinese side of this line because they were taking advantage of the Chinese cessation of patrols.[65] In all subsequent statements, the Chinese talked only in terms of line of actual control as on 7 November 1959.

However, the delegates revealed their approach to the problem and explained to the Chinese leaders how hard work they had to do to find the proposals which should be acceptable to both the countries. A joint Sino-Ceylonese statement declared that the Chinese government had given a positive response to the proposals. But the Chinese reactions were subject to two reservations; one, that the stipulation regarding Indian troops keeping their existing military positions should not apply only to the western sector but to the entire border, and second, that China would not set up civilian posts in the twenty km zone on her side of the actual line of control provided neither Indian troops nor civilians re-entered the area.

There seemed to be a snag in these Chinese reservations. While the Colombo conference acknowledged, as a substantive part of its proposals, India's right to move its forces up to the Mc Mahon line in the eastern sector, the Chinese Premier insisted that India's forces should remain at the positions to which they had been pushed back by Chinese aggression. This meant that India had to lose two areas Thagla ridge and Longju which were in its possession. Secondly, while the Colombo conference envisaged the re-establishment of the Indian presence in the area which had been under Indian control in the western sector, the Chinese Premier rejected this principle. In brief, India wanted that the status quo as of 8 September 1962 be restored. By this arrangement, China would continue to hold what was in its possession and India would regain what it had lost in the war. But this was not acceptable to China.

The Colombo proposals were discussed with the government of India in New Delhi between 11 and 13 January 1963. In responding to India's request to clarify in precise terms the Colombo proposals, the representatives of Ceylon, UAR and Ghana clearly stated that in the western sector the Chinese forces would withdraw 20 km from the line of actual control between the two sides as of 7 November 1959. The existing military posts which the forces of the government of India would retain would be those as were within the line as of 7 November. The demilitarized zone of 20 km which was up to the line created by Chinese military withdrawal would be administered by civilian posts on both sides; the location, number and composition of the posts would be decided in direct talks between India and China.

In the eastern sector the Indian forces would move right up to the south of the line of actual control, that is the Mc Mahon line with the exception of the Thagla ridge and Longju which were captured by China in the recent conflict. Similarly, the Chinese could move right up to the north of the Mc Mahon line except for these two areas. That is the Chinese would have to vacate them and go beyond them. Their future would be decided by mutual discussions between India and China.

In the middle sector, the pre-September 1962 *status quo* would be maintained and neither side would do anything to disturb it. The Chinese would withdraw from Barahoti which they had occupied in the recent war, nor would India try to reoccupy it once it was evacuated by the Chinese.

Commenting on the Colombo proposals in the Parliament Nehru pointed out to certain deficiencies which did not fully meet the Indian stand but in view of the larger interests involved in the dispute, he commended for Parliamentary approval the proposals together with the clarification offered by the Colombo conference leaders. He said, that under the proposals, except for two or three posts in south east Ladakh, Chinese forces would be withdrawn from the entire area in which Indian forward posts existed previously and in the south-eastern corner of Ladakh they would even go beyond the international boundary. Similarly Barahoti in the middle sector and Thagla in the eastern sector both of which had been under Indian control up to 8 September 1962 would not

be reoccupied by India except after negotiations with China. The future of Longuu area in the eastern sector which the Chinese had forcibly occupied for a period prior to 1962 war was also left to be settled by negotiations. As against these marginal shortcomings, Nehru pointed out that the Colombo proposals not only met the substance of India's stand but were also an improvement in the sense that a demilitarized zone would be created in the western sector instead of Indian and Chinese armed forces continuing to face each other from their old posts.[66]

The atmosphere of reconciliation that the talks between Indian and Chinese leaders on one hand and the high dignitaries of the Colombo conference on the other was short lived. Both sides reverted to the exchange of harsh notes causing much dismay to the peacemakers. Chinese President Lin Chao-chi accused India of not taking seriously the Colombo proposals which China had accepted. In his view, India wanted the six Colombo powers to assume the position of arbitrators.[67] China also complained of India's repeated incursions to the west of Spangar La. India's reply was that the area was well within its territory. China alleged that India's defence constructions were being built on the wrong side of the Nathu La pass on the Sikkim border. India protested against the establishment of a few Chinese posts south of the Karakoram pass through which access roads were being constructed. India criticised China for continuing to create the war situation in the area adjoined to Indian territory with aggressive intentions while talking of peace and friendship. China blamed India of using Sikkim as a base for intrusion into Chinese territory. In the midst of such a heated controversy, the chances of the two parties coming closer for serious discussions became remote.

However, the Ceylon Prime Minister, Mrs. Bandarnaike continued her mediatory role. During this period, a number of rumours were set afloat, one of them being that an agreement might be acceptable whereby neither side would maintain posts of any kind in the 20 km zone on the Chinese side of the line of actual control. Such a proposal was reported to have been made by two of Lord Bertrand Russel's representatives during their interviews with Nehru and Chou. The Chinese were said to be not in a mood to rule it out but they suggested that the proposals, if seriously meant, should come from Indian government itself. Nehru declared that the suggestion did not originate with him

but with the British visitors. But he believed that if the Chinese evacuated the western strip, 'the new situation...might merit consideration'.[68]

Nehru continued to believe that the solution of the problem would come out only on the basis of the Chinese unreserved acceptance of the Colombo proposals. Meanwhile, much international pressure was brought to bear upon the two countries to soften their attitude and find a via media to solve the dispute. Subsequently, when Mrs. Bandarnaike visited Peking and New Delhi in February 1964 she found both Chou and Nehru more amenable to the Colombo proposals. Chou was reported to have offered to withdraw Chinese civil posts from the demilitarized zone provided India did not insist on having its own there. Nehru agreed to have further talks only when the demilitarized zone would have posts neither of China nor of India.

In April 1964, Nehru informed the Parliament of his commitment to Mrs. Bandarnaike that if China offered to withdraw her civil posts from the demilitarized zone, India would be prepared to reciprocate this gesture. A little before his death he was more explicit in confirming that talks with China would be possible only if neither side maintained any posts in the proposed demilitarized zone in Ladakh. The Chinese did not care to respond to these gestures but went on setting up stonecairns marking the area which they had taken by force. They also started taking exception to the contacts that some individual citizens wanted to have with the people in Formosa as a leader of Swatantra party had tried to do as it amounted to tacit recognition of two Chinas by India. They also objected to the proceedings of a Moral Rearmament meeting held in Delhi which in the Chinese view was giving deliberate support to the US imperialist plot of creating two Chinas.

After the war, the Chinese, officially published maps incorporating the advanced 1960 claim line which was an extension of the 1956 claim line; west of the Karakoram, the boundary shown was that laid down by the Sino-Pak agreement a big part of which contained what was originally Indian territory. India continued to incorporate this area in its own maps though Pakistan had administered it since its illegal occupation in 1947. China's latest maps in effect, registered her military gains in 1962. On 1 March

1963 the Chinese government announced that 26 checkposts were being set up at various places along the Sino-Indian boundary including six posts in the western sector at places claimed to fall outside the area of India's 43 former posts but lying well within the 20 km belt to be demilitarized.

In military matters, the Chinese augmented their forces in Tibet so much so that the troops concentration there became much greater than at the time of aggression in October 1962. China also tried to consolidate its occupation of 14500 sq. miles of Indian territory in Ladakh. On the ground they set up stone cairns along the socalled line of actual control in Ladakh presumably to demarcate the line as if it were the international boundary. The Chinese version was that the Chinese army had made it sure that for several years to come, the *status quo* would be left undisturbed, with no more deliberate encroachments and provocative sallies from the Indian side.[69]

As a result of this debacle, Nehru had lost much of his standing in the region. When the Chinese came down into NEFA and took Tawang even Bhutan lost faith in India. Its Prime Minister Jigme Dorji came to the American ambassador to ask him for a small cut in the arms which USA might supply to India. The saving thus effected he wanted to use for his country's defence. He, no longer had any faith in Nehru's words that the 'Indian people are not people to be placated by any aggressor whoever he may be'. After the Chinese attack 'there was covert jubilation in a number of Asian capitals at India's discomfiture in the border war....Anti-Indian sentiments were quite widespread in southern Asia'.[70]

As regards the future, Indian thinking was that China may not be in a position to risk a major war as it could not be possible in view of India's preparedness with the foreign assistance it had already received and was likely to get more in case of another Chinese aggression. But confrontations in many other ways were expected like subversion in tribal region, revival of border conflicts and aggravation to India-Pak differences. Particularly after the death of Nehru, the possibility of China trying to brow beat the new weak leadership was there for the successor government to keep warned of. The war had left India so betrayed and humiliated that no halfway measures were going to lead to any tangible results

in improving the climate of Sino-Indian relationship. India had to remain content with the misfortune that had befallen her.

OBJECTIVES OF CHINESE AGGRESSION

One of the objectives of Chinese attack on India was said to be to discredit the two basic concepts of international politics, nonalignment and co-existence. In January 1963 two East European communist leaders Kardeij, the Yugoslav vice-president and Rapacki, the Polish foreign minister visited Nehru in New Delhi. They told him that what was invaded was nonalignment not India. The Chinese wanted to convince Khrushchev and other communist leaders about the hollowness and invalidity of the concept of nonalignment of which Nehru was the chief spokesman. The Chinese believed that moment a push was given to India, the whole edifice of nonalignment would crumble down and Nehru would seek shelter with the imperialist Americans. In the opinion of the two East European leaders, invasion of India was a part of the great debate between the Chinese communists and other communists in which the former did not share with the latter the belief in the nonalignment of the nonaligned countries and coexistence between communist and non-communist regimes in the world.[71]

The Chinese committed aggression not for the sake of a few patches of territory however important it could be but there was some subtle cause also. It was to destroy the image that India had come to acquire in the world and to put India in its place. There was a talk about rivalry between China and India for the leadership of Asia. Peking wanted to demonstrate to Afro-Asian nations who was the leader of Asia and where India stood. That end the Chinese could achieve by inflicting a humiliating defeat on India. Moreover, India was projected as a model country developing its economy on democratic lines. The 1962 conflict flung a spanner into India's economic development. In the Chinese eyes it served to discredit the democratic road to human progress and proved the supremacy of the communist way.

The presence of Dalai Lama in India since March 1959 and the reverential way he was treated by the Indian people may have caused annoyance among the Chinese. They may have thought that so long as the Dalai remained in India, the people in Tibet

would refuse to reconcile to the new rule of the Chinese. Some were so sensitive as to think that he, with the support of India and other like-minded nations, may stage a comeback to capture power again. In their view, a stern action against India would serve two purposes, it would quieten down the Tibetan resistance at home and would also act as a pressure on Dalai Lama to reconcile to the new realities in Tibet. To achieve this two fold objective, an aggression on India was the only course that lay before them. This is how the logic was working in the ruling circles of China.

The Chinese felt provoked by the large number of border posts which were being set up in the nature of flagposts in the territory which was Indian but which Chinese claimed was theirs. The Chinese posts were not held in one continuous line or arranged in some planned way. The Indian posts were interposed in between the Chinese posts. What further influenced the Chinese feeling was the Indian announcement which lacked veracity, that nearly 4000 sq. miles of area out of a 12000 square miles had been recaptured from the Chinese hands. Later in an unguarded moment Nehru said, 'it would be wrong to call them checkposts; they were in fact military posts'. The Chinese seized this off the cuff remark with glee. After their military successes in the 1962 war, the Chinese announced to the world that India had set up 43 strong posts; an evidence of their intention to launch an attack against China. In support they quoted Nehru's words cited above. Even our own army officers felt that mere flagposts were militarily useless and no sane military officer treated them as anything but flagposts.[72]

There was another incident which offended China. The Sino-Indian treaty on Tibet signed in 1954 was to expire in June 1962. In a way, as a protest against China's marauding exercises which resulted in the loss of territory of about 12000 sq. miles to India, New Delhi refused to extend it. Ironically it was in this agreement that the much maligned and misused Panchshila concept of five principles of peaceful coexistence first found its place. If India had agreed to extend this agreement, it would have meant that the five principles had been faithfully observed by both the sides.

Much had been made of what the Prime Minister was supposed to have said before he left for Ceylon on 12 October. On having

received the reports of Chinese intrusion at several places in Indian territory he was reported to have said: 'I have asked the army to throw the Chinese out'. It had later been said that Nehru's 'throw them out' or 'drive them out' provoked the Chinese to launch a massive attack on India before Indian army could take any step in compliance with the instructions of Nehru. It was easily forgotten that the army commanders had warned Nehru that the army was not in a position to take any such step. What he actually said was, 'our instructions are to free our country. I cannot fix a date, that is entirely for the army.' Thus it was a statement of intent not an order to be complied with. Chinese troops had entered Indian territory on 8 September, five weeks before the Prime Minister's visit to Ceylon (Sri Lanka) and they were still there. Nehru's statement merely stressed the duty that the army had to carry out whenever feasible. On his part, he was not prepared to issue definite instructions to the army without taking in view what they had to say on the situation created by the Chinese instrusions.

Let us state in brief in the end the various reasons that were given for the Chinese aggression on India. China had internal difficulties such as, (i) failure of the 'Great Leap Forward', resulting in famine and other hardships that were bound to arise in such a situation. The Chinese rulers could hold their people's faith in them by adventures abroad, (ii) China wanted, to show to the world the effectiveness of her own system of government and economic development, (iii) China wanted by an attack on India, to thwart the plans of India's economic development and to discredit her democratic structures and (iv) China wanted to show to the Soviet Union in particular that India's non involvement was a myth, that India was in reality a camp follower of the West and that, therefore the Soviet Union's policy of befriending non-aligned India was mistaken.[73]

The narrative of Chinese objectives would not be complete without taking Nehru's views into account about how this tragedy emanated. Nehru's assumption was that the Chinese had always believed that India encouraged a revolt and rebellion in Tibet. That is what ultimately turned them against us. Another reason seemed to be that China was under the impression that India was faced with many disruptive tendencies and if they gave us a blow we would split up in fragments. Moreover, to Nehru the dispute was

a conflict between two basic political ideals of peace and coexistence and our approach to socialism. From their point of view nonalignment must be attacked and destroyed first so as to remove a major obstacle that stood between the concept of world polarization and world war between the communist and capitalist block. Finally, the Chinese misfortunes in the domestic as well as foreign fields forced them to make India a whipping boy.[74]

10

POST-INVASION DEVELOPMENTS

President Ayub announced at a news conference on 23 October 1959 that Pakistan had taken initiatiave in negotiating an agreement on the 3000 mile border between Sinkiang and Azad Kashmir. The Pak foreign office had already obtained a Chinese map which showed sections of Azad Kashmir as belonging to China. The Pak overtures for negotiations repeatedly made were not accepted by China until January 1961, less than a month after the abortive Sino-Indian talks. Peking agreed in principle but no steps were taken for another year till the spring of 1962 when the Sino-Indian relations had got worsened. The two governments announced on 3 May 1962 that they would conduct their negotiations to settle their border problem. The government of India protested against this move on the plea that whatever parts of Kashmir Pakistan held under its control were its illegal occupation and as such Pakistan had no authority to barter away or negotiate any part of Indian territory.

On 26 December 1962, a day before, when the representatives of India and Pakistan were going to discuss at Rawalpindi Kashmir and other related matters the governments of China and Pakistan simultaneously announced an agreement in principle on the alignment of the border between Sinkiang and that part of Kashmir illegally occupied by Pakistan. The leader of the Indian delegation, Swaran Singh, made our position clear to President Ayub and Bhutto. In a note of protest dated 31 December 1962, the government

of India reminded the Chinese government of the latter's attempts to exploit the differences on Kashmir between Indian and Pak governments for its own designs. Pakistan could not be a party to the agreement which concerned that part of Kashmir which belonged to India. The Pak leaders were again briefed when Indo-Pak talks were resumed on 16 January 1963. The Indian government lodged a protest on 26 January against the joint communique expressing concern at Pakistan being a party to the communique.

On 22 February 1963, Pakistan government announced in a press note that the two governments of China and Pakistan had agreed to set forth in detail the boundary agreement. Accordingly the protocol was signed on 2 March 1963. Later a joint boundary demarcation commission met in Peking from 31 May to 11 June 1963. The press communique of the commission on 13 June 1963 stated that the agreement was reached on the details of demarcating the border between the two countries. The agreement was termed 'provisional' but the elaborate arrangements agreed to the appointment of a boundary commission, setting up of pillars and drawing up of protocols definitely gave it the colour of permanence. Apart from prejudicing the Indian stand regarding the traditional nature of the boundary, the very fact that Pakistan had relinquished title on a particular piece of territory which would be under Chinese control would make it impossible for India to renegotiate this position. The Pak government claimed that in this bargain they had got 700 miles of territories of occupied Kashmir. Pakistan further claimed to have gained access to six out of the seven passes along the Karakoram range and control of the three quarters of the worlds' second highest peak, Mount Gordon Austin. The Chinese on the other hand had received the territory they wanted and obtained political advantage with a view to establishing their decisive influence over the sub-continent.

As earlier stated the border agreement involved nearly 300 miles of border starting from the Karakoram pass to Pak-Afghan border. In the final agreement Pakistan claimed to have received 1350 sq. miles including 700 sq. miles of area which was in China's possession. The Chinese had been given 2050 sq. miles under the agreement. But according to Pakistan's official maps, even those published in 1962, about 11000 sq. miles of Sinkiang territory formed part of Kashmir. If one goes by these maps, Pakistan had obviously surrendered over 13000 sq. miles of territory to China.[75]

India in a note dated 10 May 1963 pointed out to the Chinese government that there was no common border between Pakistan and China and that the sovereignty over the entire Kashmir state including the part which was under Pakistan's unlawful occupation, vested solely in the Indian Union. The government of India had so far believed that China had accepted this basic position without any reservation and that China had acknowledged the final accession of the Kashmir state to the Indian union. In view of this background, China's entering into an agreement with Pakistan to negotiate the boundary of the Pak-occupied Kashmir territory was a reversal of the attitude of China in regard to India's sovereignty over the entire Kashmir territory.

China in a harsh rejoinder stated that it had never accepted the Indian stand on Kashmir without any reservation and that the Chinese government could not leave unsettled indefinitely its boundary with the areas the defence of which was under the control of Pakistan merely because there was a dispute between India and Pakistan on Kashmir. Both China and Pakistan, being sovereign states were fully entitled to conduct negotiations to settle the question of the actually existing common boundary between them. China assured that the agreement did not involve the question of the ownership of Kashmir. The agreement clearly envisaged that after the settlement of the Kashmir dispute the sovereign authorities concerned would reopen negotiations with the Chinese government on the question of the Kashmir boundary so as to conclude a formal boundary treaty to replace the provisional agreement that was going to be signed between China and Pakistan. The signing of the provisional agreement would maintain tranquility in the existing boundary between China and Pakistan and would in no way prejudice a peaceful settlement of the Kashmir dispute between India and Pakistan.

India in its note of 30 June 1963 again pointed out that there was no boundary dispute between India and China in this region which was under illegal occupation of Pakistan. The Chinese had so far given the impression on a number of occasions that they had accepted India's basic position on Kashmir. For instance, on 16 March 1956, Premier Chou En-lai told the Indian ambassador in Peking that the people of Kashmir had already expressed their will. Again on 16 July 1961 the Premier told some Indian visitors that China had not responded to the Pakistani proposal for border talks.

To emphasize his point Chou again asked: 'Can you cite any document to show that we have ever said that Kashmir is not a part of India?' Now, the note pointed out, the position has been reversed and the Chinese ask: 'Can you cite any document to show that we have ever said that Kashmir is a part of India?'

Even when Sino-Indian relations were not much strained, China began to develop close relations with Pakistan with one object in view; 'to contain the expansion of Indian influence in the region'. To Pakistan it gave a different explanation, namely, that it was to counter any security threat that India may pose to the small states of South Asia that China had to be so cautious about India. With the same logic in view, China raised no objection against Pakistan joining SEATO in 1954 and MEDO in 1955 even though the former was conceived as a bulwark against Chinese aggression on South eastern states of which Pakistan was one as the then eastern wing of Pakistan lay in this region. Pakistan claimed to have joined the pact—SEATO not out of fear of China but of India. Chou En-lai was reported to have assured the Pak delegate at Bandung conference that China had accepted the Pak version of having joined the pact to defend herself against Indian attack.[76]

In the aftermath of Chinese aggression Peking signed an agreement with Islamabad on 3 March 1963. Subsequently Pakistan was assured of all military protection in case India tried to commit any aggression on Pakistan as an attack on that country would involve the security of the entire Asia. In that case, China would not remain a silent spectator to India's aggressive designs. To give concrete form to their verbal assurance, the Chinese signed a military agreement with Pakistan in July 1966. As a result of this pact during the period 1966-70, the total Chinese military sales to Pakistan constituted 31 per cent of the 1079 million dollar arms procurement programme of Pakistan whereas the US contribution was only one per cent.[77] The magnitude of Chinese aid could be discerned from the fact that by 1970 the tanks supplied by China constituted 25 per cent of the entire tank force at the disposal of Pakistan. The aircraft supplied by China constituted 31 per cent of Pakistan's air force, 65 per cent of all inceptor bombers and 99 per cent of it modern the fighter planes.

The opening of the Karakoram highway in June 1978, linking Kinjiwang to Gilgit, further facilitated the movement of arms to

ocean. Thus the north west region of China had got direct access to the sea through this highway. The Climax of Sino-Pakistan relations was reached when on 30 June 1966 the two countries signed an agreement on nuclear cooperation. The cooperation between the two countries in nuclear field had developed in plutonium reprocessing and uranium enrichment through the centrifuge method by 1978 and by 1984 Pakistan had actually developed the capability to design nuclear weapons.[78]

CHINA'S ATOM BOMB

China exploded her first nuclear device on 16 October 1964. It was clear that Peking may not use it but it was meant to intimidate all non-nuclear states. China did this to coincide with the conference of nonaligned nations at Cairo in early October. But China failed to set off the blast in time to influence the conference. Soviet Union did likewise in 1961 a little before the first nonaligned conference met in Belgrade. Nehru with President of Ghana Nkrumah was deputed to go to Moscow to convey the sentiments of the nonaligned countries. China probably expected the same gesture from the conference but this idea was ruled out as not befitting the significance of the occasion as also China was not expected to be courteous enough to discuss this issue seriously.

Nevertheless, Prime Minister Shastri in his first important initiative in international affairs had attempted to rally those powers into a force to halt proliferation of nuclear weapons. Addressing the Cairo conference on 7 October he proposed that a delegation of nonaligned nations visit Peking to 'persuade China to desist from making nuclear weapons'. Shastri's[79] proposal was not accepted by the conference and he dropped the idea.

China in a strong anti-Indian rejoinder attacked India which clearly indicated that the attempt to halt nuclear armament had become another reason for increased Chinese pressure on India. The Chinese repeated a number of old charges in an attempt to belittle India before the conference and accused the country of double alignment in accepting arms from both Russia and the US.

Within India, the explosion created renewed pressure for the

development of an independent Indian nuclear device. Shastri had already declared at Cairo that India would not join in the race of nuclear proliferation. But since the demand was made in the context of a new development, it had some impact on the public opinion. There was another snag in it. If India had developed its nuclear capacity it would appear to many foreigners that it was directed against Pakistan and not China.

On the day of Chinese explosion Shastri said in the Parliament, "China has been trying to build herself a mighty war machine. The atom bomb is the latest type of weapon which cuts across a general desire of humanity to live in peace. I do hope that the voice of the peaceloving people in all countries will be raised against it and the world conscience awakened to fight this aggression on peace and security."

INDO-PAK WAR

During the 1965 Indo-Pak war there came about a strong collusion between Pakistan and China because both wanted to settle old scores with India. On 4 September 1965 Peking's foreign minister Chen Yi utilised his brief stopover in Karachi to have a six-hour talk with Bhutto. The Chinese minister was reported to have given an oblique support to Pakistan in the latter's just action that it might have to take to expel India's armed provocation. This was taken clearly as evidence that Peking was sure of a war breaking out between India and Pakistan and in that case the Chinese would support Pakistan against Indian aggression. On 5 September when Pakistan launched its massive offensive to capture Kashmir, Peking was first silent but when the tide began to turn against Pakistan it started threatening India. But it was the western and Soviet Premier that silenced China and contributed to the cessation of hostilities.[80]

On 8 September when the impact of the Pak armoured counter offensive began to be felt on the Punjab front, the Chinese lodged the first of a series of border threats against India. China accused India of violating the Sikkim border on several occasions in the past two months and demanded the halt of further 'provocations'. It warned that 'India must bear the responsibility for the consequences ensuing therefrom'. The note further continued that India had

continued to intrude on Chinese territory since 1962 and that Indian aggression against any one of its neighbours would concern all its neighbours. In some political circles in Pakistan it was believed that they expected direct Chinese assistance in the form of diversionary action.

Soon after midnight on 17 September, the Indian envoy in Peking was given an ultimatum. There was no direct reference in it to the war with Pakistan but the timing made that formality unnecessary. The note said that India must destroy the bunkers that it had constructed along the Sikkim border or face counter action by China. To this threat was added the ridiculous charge that Indians had stolen some of the Chinese Yaks.

The protest note was referred to the Prime Minister Lal Bahadur Shastri who with utmost poise and coolest display of nerves simply announced that any threat by China would be resolutely met. An exchange of shots between boundary forces both in Sikkim and Ladakh, further prompted Shastri to make this remark. The Chinese would have read the Indian mind through the words of Shastri. The Chinese also knew that the US had already warned them to stay out of the Indo-Pak war. They knew any move on their part against India would result in American retaliation. Moscow through *Tass* had also warned that 'no government had the right to add fuel to the fire' and if anybody did that, 'it would have a grave responsibility'.[81]

The Chinese ultimatum giving notice of three days to India was further extended to the five-day time limit with a statement implying that India had sent a conciliatory reply. The Indian reply, however, was anything but conciliatory. As regards the 'abducted' live stock, some Indian parties paraded a flock of 800 sheep in front of the Chinese embassy in Delhi. Some of them carried posters around their neck: 'Eat us but save the world; don't start a war, we are here'. On 22 September, Peking announced that the Indians had complied with their demands for dismantling the disputed structures. If they were destroyed, according to an Indian spokesman, the Chinese must have done it themselves.

The UN resolutions of 20 September urged the cessation of hostilities. Bhutto confirmed that the Chinese pressure was responsible for including in the UN resolution, the clause pledging future consideration of a political solution for the Kashmir problem. As reported in the London *Times* on 6 October 1965, Bhutto added;

'the Chinese ultimatum to India had shaken the UN and the great powers into realizing the danger of war on the subcontinent and that only a political settlement would allow permanent peace'. Ayub announcing the ceasefire said, 'the moral support which the Chinese government extended to us so willingly and so generously will for ever remain enshrined in our hearts. We are grateful to them.'

India did not apprehend a large overt Chinese attack on the 1962 pattern but the government was concerned over any diversionary action. Premier Shastri was reported to have told the US ambassador, Chester Bowles, that India expected limited military hostilities on the India-China border for which they were prepared. In case it assumed the form of a big war, prompt intervention by big powers particularly the US was expected. This time the USSR would also take a more forthright stand in not only warning but also threatening China from taking such an ill conceived step.

In general it was believed in India that the Chinese were seeking some excuse to start their aggressive activities in collusion with its new ally—Pakistan. It was also assumed in some political circles that Peking was attempting to stiffen Pakistan's resolve to continue the conflict with India. The extension of the time limit for dismantling the military posts on the Indo-Sikkim border was a device to gain time to watch what came out of the discussion in the Security Council. This probably meant that Peking was prepared for more vigorous action if Pakistan rejected the UN resolution on ceasefire. In case, it accepted the UN directive to ceasefire, Peking on its part could feel satisfied as the onus would be on Peking to justify its action.

It was also possible that China felt obliged to make some non-committal gesture at the last minute to compensate for its inability to actively support Pakistan during the period of hostilities despite the latter's repeated appeals. The most China could do was to indulge in high blown propaganda to keep the Indian forces at the border in alert. A bolder demonstration was required which Peking could not provide because they were more interested in minimizing their involvement by waiting until the closing days of the conflict rather than by indulging in some violent interlude. China was more anxious to see that Pakistan did not reject the UN resolution otherwise the Chinese would be more obliged to help Pakistan in some other way. Pakistan felt disappointed because their

government had initially rejected the UN proposal for a ceasefire in the hope that the Chinese ultimatum, about which they knew in advance, would have a deterrent influence on India. But it turned out to be a damp squib. The main effective deterrent to Chinese aggressive designs was the possibility of American intervention which could dash all Chinese hopes.

Pakistan in the end agreed to accept UN proposal for ceasefire because of the inadequacy of ammunition stocks and spare parts for US supplied equipment. The US had already declared embargo on American arms to both India and Pakistan but as the latter's armoury was mostly America supplied, it had to suffer more than India who hardly had any arms dealing with America. Moreover, it was also getting obvious that Peking's threatening posture served only to provoke irresistible pressure of the US and USSR for a ceasefire. Thus the Chinese instigation to Pakistan became more of an embarrassment than a help. It is worth noting that of all the countries involved in the crisis, China was the only one to feel unhappy with the Tashkent agreement signed on 11 January 1966 between India and Pakistan at the initiative of the Soviet Union. The Chinese probably wanted the hostilities to continue so that they would continue to fish in the troubled waters of Indian subcontinent and also because a prolonged conflict would weaken India militarily as well as economically.

China by its indiscree. behaviour failed to achieve its objective of humiliating India but also lost its face among the Afro-Asian community. China's role wrecked the 'Bandung' spirit of Afro-Asian solidarity so hopefully enunciated in April 1955 at Bandung conference in Indonesia. The second Bandung conference was rescheduled to take place on 5 November 1965 at Algiers and Peking was its principal promoter. Its main aim was to exploit it as an international forum for asserting its leadership claim in the Afro-Asian world. But China's abortive intrusion into Indo-Pak war in 1965 and its questionable role in instigating a pro-Peking communist coup in Indonesia, which also took place on the eve of the Algiers conference, created an atmosphere of hostility which China could not have faced without being embarrassed at the Algiers conference. China had no option left but to get the Algiers conference cancelled with the help of a few of its allies.[82]

11

BANGLADESH CRISIS: CHINESE REACTIONS

The Chinese, more than any other people, were, from the very beginning, deeply involved in the Bangladesh crisis. Probably they realised, more than others, the strategic and diplomatic importance of keeping Pakistan as their ally on this issue. With Pakistan to their side, the Chinese thought, they would be able to face more easily their dominant neighbour, India. The geographical position of Pakistan was of special advantage for China. Since the mainland of India lay, between the two wings of Pakistan, China could create trouble for India in the west as well as in the east.[83]

BACKGROUND

There is a story about what the true sentiments of the Chinese were towards Bengalis and their political aspirations in pre-liberation days. In March 1971 when the Chinese technicians were building an ordnance factory in the then East-Pakistan Bengali workers went on strike to press some of their demands. The martial law administration threatened stringent action against the striking Bengali workers but when the Chinese personnel also chose to stay away from work, the Pakistani authorities felt embarrassed and had to yield to their demands.[84] The authorities took it as a 'non-neutral' behaviour on the part of Chinese as it amounted to interference in the domestic matters of Pakistan. Further, there were

reports that certain sections of the pro-Peking East Pakistani communists had been in touch with the Chinese agents in neighbouring Nepal. These communists had been demanding an armed revolt to create an independent Bangladesh.

CHINESE INSCRUTABLE SILENCE

The Chinese in the beginning were quite reserve about the happenings in Bangladesh, no press comments were available as if the matter seemed to be a taboo. The Chinese diplomats were asked to treat this issue as an internal affair of Pakistan and China did not believe in interfering in the internal affairs of other countries. This was a strange stand because after Albania, the Indo-Chinese countries and North Korea, Pakistan belonged to the circle of close friends of China in whose affairs China took a special interest for political, economic and strategic reasons. Towards Pakistan, the Chinese consistently showed unusual warmth. Only in the preceding November (1970) they had played host lavishly to Yahya Khan. They gave liberally all help that Pakistan could utilise including a $ 300 million interest free loan for development projects. Besides, the Chinese engineers and technicians had built roads and plants and brought the much needed technical know-how to Pakistan.

But the upheaval in Bangladesh presented China with a diplomatic dilemma. The Chinese dilemma stemmed from its efforts to cultivate closer relations with Pakistan and its strong commitments to support the revolution and forces of liberation. The Bangladesh movement could be seen in Maoist terms as a classic case of a peasant revolutionary movement against an oppressive reactionary military dictatorship. Now they were confronted with the same type of liberation movement Peking had been advocating so strongly since the Chinese claimed their capital was the true centre of world revolution. But China like any other country was determined not to be guided by the ideological commitments so much as by considerations of national interest.

China wanted an occasion which could provide it with an excuse to give vent to its resentment over Indian policy towards Bangladesh. Such a pretext was provided when on 29 March some Indian citizens organised a peaceful demonstration outside the

Chinese embassy in Delhi in protest against the use of Chinese arms by the Pakistani army in Bangladesh and refuelling facilities provided by Peking for Pakistani planes flying troops to Bangladesh. China sent a protest note on 6 April in which it criticised the 'participants' for having 'slandered' China by 'accusing Peking of helping the Pakistani government in its war against the freedom-loving people of East Bengal'. 'At present while flagrantly interfering in the internal affairs of Pakistan, the Indian government has gone so far as to connive with the wilful trouble-making by Indians in front of the China Embassy,' the note of protest observed. India rejected the Chinese protest and repudiated the insinuation against the Indian government with the statement that none had intruded into the Chinese embassy. It also suggested that Peking had no reason to meddle in Indo-Pakistani relations as what was happening in Bangladesh was a popular upsurge against Islamabad's repressive policies.[85]

A question often posed was: did New Delhi ever care to tell Peking of what was happening in Bangladesh? Indian answer was given in Parliament (Rajya Sabha) on 7 April when the deputy minister of external affairs stated that India had not conveyed to the Chinese government India's views on the happenings in East Bengal. The Chinese were expected to know them. 'Since we have not directly conveyed to them our views the question of their reaction does not arise', the Minister clinched the issue. But what remained an enigma for India was what sort of understanding Yahya had with Peking before embarking on the military misadventure in East Bengal to ensure himself against the remote possibility of Indian intervention.

CHINESE REACTIONS

The first Chinese reaction to Bangladesh crisis was witnessed when through its press media it attacked Podgorny's appeal to Yahya Khan to come to terms with the political leaders of East Bengal. The *People's Daily* in its issue of 11 April criticised it as an uncalled for interference by the Soviet government in the affairs which concerned Pakistan government alone. Such a communication was called one-sided affair which would cause resentment in Pakistan and encourage India to be aggressive towards Pakistan.

This was followed by Chou's message of comfort and assurance to protect Pakistan from any external aggression. The message, in part, read: 'In our opinion the unification of Pakistan and the unity of the people of East and West Pakistan are the basic guarantees for Pakistan to attain prosperity and strength'. Chou's message admitted that what was happening in Pakistan should get settled without any outside interference. It also criticised India for 'gross interference in the internal affairs of Pakistan by exploiting the internal problems of the country.

Further, the message assured Pakistan that 'if Indian expansionists dare to launch aggression against Pakistan, the Chinese government and people will, as always, firmly support the Pakistan government and people in their just struggle to safeguard state sovereignty and national independence. Simultaneously, China agreed to give a $ 70 million loan to Pakistan to finance some of its badly needed imports. This aid was to be given out of the $ 300 million loan announced by China in November 1970 for Pakistani current development programme. Finally, it was at this time that Chou's proposed visit to Pakistan was announced before the commencement of the UN General Assembly session in September 1971. But it did not materialise probably because of the deteriorating political situation in Pakistan.

It seems that subsequently two factors brought home to Peking the truth of the crisis. First, the junta had so alienated itself from the people of Bangladesh that political palliatives were unlikely to work. Second, the world wide revulsion against the West Pakistani atrocities was so strong that China by aligning itself with Pakistan would lose world sympathy. These developments made China cautious and somewhat realist in its approach. Despite these considerations, it was reported that China started by mobilising its troops to the extent to ten crack divisions along Sino-Indian border in the eastern sector. The concentration of Chinese troops assumed significance in the context of communist China's stand on the bloody struggle in East Bengal. The Indian government was aware of the danger it posed.

The Chinese news media from the very beginning tried to broadcast all over the world that what was happening in East Bengal was a mere civil disorder created by a dissatisfied section of the

people and India was instigating the trouble makers with a view to causing disintegration of Pakistan. The Chinese claimed to be the staunch supporters and unfailing friends of small and weak nations. And Pakistan was certainly such a country, more so when compared to India, a country five times as large. And what Peking was doing was to help and protect Pakistan against an indirect aggression of India. Such a stand irrespective of its merit might prove to be a solace to many others who might likewise feel in need of such a help. This appeared to be a more attractive offer when viewed as the help given by a communist country to an avowedly non-communist country like Pakistan who was known for its blatantly reactionary regime. Moreover, some countries of this region were likely to believe in Peking propaganda which was that the Chinese believed in absolute equality of all nations and in the policy of peaceful coexistence which meant that each country, big or small, had every right to live its own way of life without interference from outside.

There was a snag in this way of arguing the Chinese case. So far, every country in the region of Southeast Asia feared only one trouble and that was from China, either overtly as direct aggression or covertly, which was the usual pattern followed so far, namely, internal uprising created by the local Chinese population. China had not come forward to help any country suppress the trouble created by its own adherents. All these unsavoury facts of Chinese behaviour were likely to be forgotten in the midst of loud promises that were being made by Peking to help Pakistan. It was not a help to Pakistan for its own sake but an assistance to an enemy of India. So it was one enemy of India helping another enemy for its own benefit. In short range objective it was to hamper post-election prospects of a stable and progressive India; and in its long range aim it was to help Pakistan to retain its identity as a counterpoise against India. In both, China seemed to have failed.

Why did not China generously support Bangladesh revolution? This was the question many people all over the world posed particularly when they recollected that China had always proclaimed itself as a leader of anti-imperialist camp and friend and supporter of national liberation movements the world over. What was intriguing was that with the exception of China, all the other communist countries and parties of the region, North Vietnam,

North Korea, the Pathet Lao and the Viet Cong, remained neutral in this conflict, neither condemning India nor supporting Pakistan. Equally noteworthy was the attitude of Prince Norodom Sihanouk who also took no sides in the war despite the fact that he was a guest of China. At one time he praised the Indian government for taking without much resentment the refugee problem created by the developments in Bangladesh. He did so despite the fact that the Indian government had not recognised his government in exile. The reasons for non-communist governments' neutral attitude was that they had cordial relations with both Pakistan and India. The reason why the communist countries had refrained from commenting was that there was on one hand, China, which was committed to support Pakistan, as its ally and on the other there were 75 million people who were justifiably engaged in a struggle for liberation.

One cynical explanation that could be given about China was that the guerrillas of the Mukti Bahini had only a gun in their hands and no Little Red Book of Mao's thoughts in their pockets to make them acceptable to Peking as revolutionary guerrillas. To deserve Peking help, the revolution should be demonstrably Marxist-Leninist. Any other uprising, with however plausible motives it may be launched, would not command Chinese support. In all other cases Chinese would support the governments in power, whatever their character, against popular minority or even class uprising. The governments in Sudan, Ceylon and Pakistan have been the recent examples of having been recipients of Chinese help for suppressing thoroughly revolutionary movements that broke out in these countries. This is the way how China tried to win favour of the third world countries. However, in case of Bangladesh Awami League was considered by Peking as a bourgeoisie led party working in collusion with India and as such it was susceptible to Indian and Soviet influences. But a section of the Maoists believed that as a bourgeoisie-led movement it could not be sustained for long and in the final analysis it would move towards Maoist policies and methods.

Keeping this long-range view of the movement in mind the Chinese should have helped the Bangladesh movement. But they preferred to remain indifferent. Peking ignored the fact that the Bangladesh movement was a manipulation of anti-colonial

nationalism and as such it could not be alienated by neglect. This was also forgotten that this movement had attracted to its fold Marxist-communists friendly to Peking. In brief, the whole tenor of Peking argument was essentially fallacious and based on distorted facts so much so that even Indian Marxists found the pill too bitter to swallow easily.

Another strange aspect of China's argument was that the uprising in Bangladesh which resulted in the exodus of over ten million refugees to India was analogous to what Peking had pictured to be the India-inspired uprising in Tibet and the influx of Tibetan refugees into India. This was the first time that China had officially admitted that the uprising in Tibet which it had suppressed was similar to the uprising in Bangladesh. The Chinese had a purpose in confusing the issue by linking it with the plight of the refugees from Tibet in 1959. There was a possibility that the Tibetan issue might be raised in the UN as a human rights issue and so China was trying to build up a case to forestall such a move. Otherwise this analogy between Tibet and Bangladesh had no other relevance. Moreover, how fantastic the Chinese were when they felt that if India was able to establish the Bangladesh government firmly in Dacca it may along with Russia encircle China and eventually try to 'liberate' Tibet for the Dalai Lama. They charged that India made the presence of East Bengal refugees on its soil a pretext for launching military action against Pakistan and might justify a similar operation against Tibet on similar grounds.

No doubt the disturbed situation on Indo-Pak frontiers on China's south west flank was perhaps the principal preoccupation of Chinese leaders, but they were out of their mind in believing that the liberation of Bangladesh would be a prelude to the invasion of Tibet by India or of Sinkiang by the Soviet Union. The Chinese were devoid of common sense when they gave military aid to Pakistan on the understanding that if Pakistan was given arms and encouraged to expand in Kashmir sector they would have less to worry about in the border regions near India. India had no designs on any part of Chinese territory. India's objective was very limited, namely, to get the refugee problem solved amicably.

In making such allegations the Chinese seemed to have forgotten

that it was Pakistan which had attacked India on 3 December and India struck back only in self-defence. Secondly, there was no parallel between the situation in Tibet and the situation that prevailed in East Bengal. The Tibetans came to India because they could not adjust their religious life with the Chinese communist way of life. They were given refuge as religious exiles not as political refugees. The atrocities committed by the West Pakistani army in East Bengal were of an entirely different category. Over nine million refugees were forced to come to India to create serious economic problems for us whereas a few thousand Tibetan refugees could hardly make any adverse effect on our economic life. This should also be kept in mind that India recognised Tibet as an integral part of China in 1954 and continued to recognise it as such. It is the continuing border dispute between India and China and not the situation in Tibet or the activities of the Dalai Lama or other Tibetan refugees in India which had prevented normalisation of Sino-Indian relations.

During the crisis it was often argued that Chinese could not be sympathetic towards East Bengal's demand for autonomy or independence because the Chinese themselves could not settle their minority problem as satisfactorily as Russia had done. The Soviet Union had from the very beginning provided in their constitution a right to all federating units to secede freely from the Union. To avoid facing any such embarrassing demand the Chinese have never conceded the right of self-determination to the tribal and other minority nationalists which are under their control. Still the Chinese often feel worried on this account and often show anxiety over Sinkiang where even after many centuries of Chinese domination the Uighurs and the Kazhaks are yet to identify themselves fully with Peking. There are also indications that Tibet's emotional integration with the People's Republic is far from being complete.

WHY DID CHINA HELP PAKISTAN?

The Chinese felt that Pakistan had been a consistent friend of China for the last 17 years despite changes of government. They recalled rather gratefully that during the entire period of Sino-Soviet rift Pakistan stood with China. In support of their belief, they gave concrete examples of Pakistani acts of friendliness. One story was

about 1962 when China mounted attack on both sides – northeast as well as northwest – of Indian border. America came to India's help but keeping in mind that the help given should be so limited as may not annoy Pakistan the assistance given was very meagre. In a confidential communication Kennedy requested Ayub Khan to make a friendly gesture towards India. As a concrete step he suggested that Ayub Khan should privately inform Nehru that Indian troops posted in Kashmir could be safely withdrawn and deployed elsewhere to fight against the Chinese divisions. Theodore Sorenson, the biographer of Kennedy, says that American President made this suggestion hoping that such a gesture would evoke very generous Indian response in settling Kashmir problem. Ayub Khan did not accept this proposal. His lack of assurance to India helped Peking at that hour. China had not forgotten this incident.

Another incident relates to the very recent past. In July 1971 it was through the good offices of Yahya Khan that Nixon's adviser Kissinger could make a secret trip to Peking where he discussed the prospects of American President's visit to China. In this connection the entire strategy was so neatly organised by Yahya Khan himself that till the last moment Kissinger's flight remained a closely guarded secret. This cooperation made the trip a success for America for which Nixon had paid handsome compliments to Yahya Khan. The Chinese also must have felt grateful to Yahya for helping them to come closer to America.

A major factor which led to the Chinese decision to help Pakistan was its desire to counter Soviet influence in neighbouring countries. Chinese criticism of India was linked to alleged encouragement of New Delhi by 'socialist imperialism' which had entered into a treaty of friendship with India. The Chinese leaders were telling the world community that India was playing in the Russian hands and that a weak Pakistan may mean Indo-Soviet hegemony in the Indian sub-continent.

Secondly, the Chinese decided to side with Pakistan because of the fear of a credibility gap arising between Peking and its allies if at this time it failed to help Pakistan. For the last several years Pakistan was generally considered a close friend and ally of China and any hesitation on China's part to support Pakistan at this critical juncture would have led to a devaluation of Chinese pledges among

its limited number of friends. Moreover, China had to keep in mind how great were the returns with which Pakistan repaid Chinese aid. Like the US, China also supplied arms to Pakistan. In return for its aid, China got two principal benefits from Yahya Khan. First, Pakistan provided one of China's two major airlinks with the world. Lacking long-range jets, China had for long relied on foreign airlines for its delegations' trip abroad. Travel via Pakistan was the only alternative to travel via the Soviet Union which the Chinese had earlier followed.[86] Pakistan met this air-transport need of China. Secondly, China's influence in Pakistan had enabled it to maintain a balance against the Soviet Union which had developed friendly relations with India. China has been traditionally anxious to have good relations with its neighbours particularly with Pakistan which it wanted to use as a counter-weight to India as the latter had become much disillusioned with China since 1962 border-conflict.

Short of armed intervention, China gave all possible help to Pakistan to carry on its war against Bangladeshi people. About 100 lorries came from China to Pakistan daily through the recently completed Sinkiang-Gilgit highway. They carried military stores to equip additional units of Pakistani army which had taken the place of units already despatched to East Pakistan as the latter might have to stay in the east as an army of occupation for an indefinite period. Secondly, the lorries also carried Chinese commercial commodities for export to African countries through Karachi port.

This was a welcome source of revenue to Pakistan which was faced with a serious foreign exchange crisis resulting from the disruption of industry and trade in East Bengal. Thirdly, Chinese had given overflight and staging facilities for Pakistani troop flights from West Pakistan to East Bengal. It was reported that Pakistani aircrafts with supplies to reinforce troop operations in Bangladesh were flying via Urunchi in Sinkiang province of China. According to press reports, massacre in Bengal began on the day a Chinese ship unloaded arms and ammunition in Chittagong despite protests by port workers and Awami League volunteers.[87] Finally, according to press reports, 200 Chinese guerrilla warfare experts were flown to Bangladesh to train Pakistani forces. The experts came in the wake of mounting Mukti Bahni attack in Mymensing sector during the third week of October. The experts were sent by Peking in

response to an urgent appeal by Yahya Khan. Twenty training camps, each comprising 250 Pakistani soldiers and ten Chinese instructors were reportedly set up in the forests near Dacca.

In spite of all the supply of arms and other gestures of helpfulness it was almost certain that China would at no cost actively involve itself in Indo-Pakistani conflict should one erupt nor did it want to escalate tension in the sub-continent for it knew well that the moment it stepped in the Russians would also come in. It would have been quite another story, however, if Russia had first intervened on the side of India. Even in such a situation, China would have plunged into the fray only when America had preceded it. To think that Russia would enter the conflict unprovoked was to misunderstand the Russian diplomatic thinking. Russia was determined to keep aloof unless forced to intervene by American or Chinese intervention.

Another reason why China could not get itself involved in any Indo-Pak conflict was that its involvement would bring New Delhi and Moscow closer which would be very adverse to the Chinese interests. The fact that the Soviet Union and India were the only two countries which had not yet signed border agreements with China made both suspect in Peking eyes as natural accomplices. Moreover, the Soviet declaration, however obliquely it expressed to defend India's frontiers, seemed to have been interpreted by the Chinese as a counter commitment on the part of New Delhi to respect the Soviet borders. China's obvious fear was that if it got involved itself in an Indo-Pakistani war Russia would strike somewhere along the 4500-mile frontier. Chinese had it fresh in mind that in the spring in 1969 the two countries had fought a pitched battle for the disputed territory along the Amu-Ussuri rivers in Central Asia. The Soviet strength along the disputed border with China had trebled in three years, the number of Soviet divisions having increased from 15 in 1968 to 44 in 1971.

In brief, China had two common complaints against India and Russia. These two countries had not settled their border disputes with China whereas the latter had settled this issue with all neighbours having common frontiers with China. Secondly, these countries had been accused of subversion in China. India instigated a trouble in Tibet in 1959 and the Soviet Union in 1963 engineered

a rebellion in Sinkiang and several thousand civilians fled to Russia and were still in Soviet land as Tibetans were in India.[88]

PRIME MINISTER'S LETTER

In mid-July, the Prime Minister wrote a letter to Chou En-lai about the developments in Bangladesh. The Chinese leader did not care to send a reply. It may be because the letter was sent to the Chinese Premier in July only when Kissinger had already visited China; whereas to other heads of state a communication of this nature was sent in May. The Chinese might have felt ignored and slighted and did not feel to be in a hurry to send an acknowledgement of this letter. It was also reported that the Chinese were presumably planning to acknowledge receipt of Mrs. Gandhi's letter probably with some comments when India had signed the treaty with Russia. The Chinese seemed to have felt a little puzzled by Indian government's unusual diplomatic posture. On one hand Mrs. Gandhi had sent a letter to Chou En-lai seeking his good offices on Bangladesh crisis, on the other, she simultaneously rushed her emissary to Moscow to finalise arrangements to sign an Indo-Soviet treaty. In such a situation Peking thought it proper to sit tight over the matter.

Another reason put forward on behalf of the Chinese, why their Prime Minister did not reply to Mrs. Gandhi's letter on Bangladesh, was that he did not want to involve his country in an affair which he considered to be a matter to be resolved between the two neighbours. But the Chinese had revealed their mind to several foreigners that while China sympathised with India for the immense problems it was facing as a result of the refugee influx from East Bengal, it could not possibly tell President Yahya how to run his country. Besides, any suggestion to Gen. Yahya on an issue which concerned his country would run counter to the Chinese non-intervention policy and amount to an interference in the internal affairs of another country. Further, China did not want to give an impression to Pakistan that its friendship was no longer required because of its desire to revive old cordiality towards India. This may have been the impression in Pak political circles if China had cared to send an early reply to Mrs. Gandhi's letter. In fact, China could continue to strengthen its friendship with Pakistan despite the fact that Peking did not approve of Islamabad's policy in all matters.

CHINA AND THE INDO-SOVIET TREATY

China, quite understandably, did not take kindly to the treaty and its subsequent criticism was an indication of the stand it was going to take on Bangladesh crisis. Accordingly, in his interview to Reston, an American journalist, Chou En-lai accused India of conspiring with the Soviet Union to dismember Pakistan. But later the Chinese adopted a soft line. A seven-member communist China's trade delegation led by the vice-minister for foreign trade, Chou Hua-ming, went on a seven day visit to Guyana in the last week of August 1971. The spokesman of the delegation at a press conference on 3 September 1971 in referring to the treaty said that China certainly did not regard the signing of the Indo-Soviet friendship treaty as a friendly act so far as it was concerned. He observed that China was watching what he called the growing USSR-India collaboration against China. Later Chou revealed his mind in another way when he said that the treaty had much to do with the announcement of Nixon's visit to China. This was announced on 15 July 1971 and the treaty was signed on 9 August. Chou in an interview to Neville Maxwell of the *Times* (London) said on 20 November that the draft of the treaty had remained shelved in the coffers of the Soviet ministry of foreign affairs for two years and it would have remained there for an indefinite period. But the announcement of Nixon's visit to China spurred the Soviets to come out with this treaty and formally sign it with India.

Despite all these presumptions, the Chinese seemed to have remained quite clear in one thing, namely, that this treaty had placed India in a very anomalous position, outwardly independent but actually dependent on the Soviet Union in international matters. In actual operation, they thought, the treaty would bring India under excessive influence of the Soviet Union which would not allow India to make independent moves for improving relations with China. To the Chinese, it seemed to be the first step towards realising Brezhnev's Asian collective security system which was directed against the countries towards which Russia was hostile. This could not materialize because the other countries to which the Soviet Union had approached with this idea had refused to accept it.[89]

This was believed in some quarters that China would not have been so categorical in its support for Pakistan had India not signed this treaty with the Soviet Union. In its ultimate analysis, this treaty brought China and Pakistan closer to each other—an eventuality which India in its own interest would have not allowed to happen. But the truth was the other way round. China should have realised the fact that it was mostly responsible for creating a situation in which India was left with no other alternative but to go in for this alliance. For the last several years India had been trying to create conditions in which the Sino-Indian relations would have improved but China's defiant attitude left no alternative for India but to seek Soviet friendship. Moscow also felt outdone by China's agreeing to receive Kissinger and discuss with him the prospects of Nixon's visit. After that Moscow became keen to take some Asian initiative to counter the effect of China's opportunistic diplomacy. And the treaty was the first move.

ANALYSIS OF CHINA'S STAND

It was usually felt that China's opposition to the Bangladesh struggle on one hand and support to Emperor Haile Silassie of Ethiopia and its friendliness to the new Sudanese regime that had suppressed communist sponsored insurgency on the other were inconsistent with the creed of communism which China professed to practise. In Bangladesh crisis China's action had to be viewed as being motivated by geo-political interests to override ideological considerations and needs of national liberation struggles. Earlier also China had shown much interest in Czechoslovakia not on some principles but because it was motivated solely by a desire to embarrass the Soviet Union, its chief political adversary. Again, it is Pakistan that had launched a pre-emptive attack on India on 3 December and not India on Pakistan. In this case, China's another adversary India was in trouble to exploit which China got an opportunity in the attack by Pakistan.

However, in this context, another point had to be kept in view, namely, that it was India alone that was affected by the refugee problem and not China or America. Again, every effort was made by India to arouse world conscience to what was happening in its neighbouring country but all turned their blind eye towards what was going to be the most explosive situation in the sub-continent.

For nine long months India waited to see that either Pakistan resolved the crisis or its allies helped to bail it out of the chaos it had created for itself as well as for India. How unaware India was caught is clear from the fact that neither the Prime Minister nor any of her two senior ministers was in the capital on the day Pakistani aircrafts bombarded six Indian airports.

BHUTTO MISSION

A high power delegation led by Bhutto was sent by Yahya Khan to visit Peking from 5 to 8 November 1971 with the object which was not made clear even by the government of Pakistan itself. A Pakistani military delegation had visited Peking in early May and in June China had sent arms and ammunitions for the two divisions intended for action and built an arms plant. Moreover, in 1970 several Pakistani leaders had been to China including Air Marshal Rahim Khan, Vice-Admiral Muzaffar Hussain, Lt. Gen. Atiqur Rehman and lastly, Yahya Khan himself. So its object could not be only to seek arms aid though three military generals were included in the delegation. The timing of the delegation's visit was significant in that it coincided with Mrs. Gandhi's visit to Washington. Pakistan had earlier tried to see that Mrs. Gandhi's tour did not come off. Pakistan started intensifying troops movements and dispersal of Pakistani forces on the entire Indo-Pakistani border with a view to creating a situation of crisis so that India might be panicked into taking similar steps and the Prime Minister might cancel her foreign tour. Having failed in that move, Pakistan sent a high-powered delegation to Peking to divert public attention from the Prime Minister's tour to Pakistani manoeuvring in Peking.[90]

It was believed in some quarters in India that before announcing the visit of Bhutto mission to Peking, Yahya Khan had taken Nixon into confidence and secured his approval to such a diplomatic move. Apparently the object of this prior consultation was to show that Pindi did not want to make any move towards China without consulting Washington in advance. It was quite understandable for Yahya to do so because he wanted to ensure American readiness to Pakistan's help along with China's support. He could not afford to lose the good will of either. Presumably, Washington would have allowed Pindi to go ahead with the mission as it would act as a

timely warning to India that China was not going to remain a silent spectator to the current developments in the subcontinent though America may not take any step against India. It was a clear threat on the part of America to demoralise Indian people. Americans further tried to reinforce this threat by an announcement made in Islamabad a day earlier that a Pakistani merchant ship had already left for China for bringing artillery mortars, vehicles and other ammunitions for Chinese tanks already in use in Pakistan. So it appeared to be a part of war of nerves jointly manoeuvred by America and China to frighten India; a reminder of what Kissinger had already said that India must not count on American assistance if it ran into trouble with China again.

The purpose of the mission had to be viewed as a move in the war of nerves to offset, to some extent, the impression created by the visits paid by a number of Soviet leaders including the chief of Soviet air force to India. A little before the delegation left, Yahya Khan had given two identical interviews to the American news magazine, *News Week* and *London Daily Mail*, the purport of which was that the Chinese would help Pakistan in the event of an aggression committed by India. In making this statement he had two ends in view: first, that he wanted to let the world know that Pakistan would not be deserted by its Chinese friends in an hour of trial and that it should serve as a warning to India; secondly, it was to act as a morale booster to the people of Pakistan whose morale was already sagging. A gesture was needed at such a time to hearten the people so that they could feel that Pakistan too had friends whom its leaders could approach in time of need.

It was also believed in some quarters that Bhutto had in his mind the idea of having a defence pact with China on the lines of the Indo-Soviet treaty of 9 August 1971. But it may be asked: was there a possibility of such a pact between China and Pakistan? So far, China had not signed any treaty of mutual defence assistance in the sense that an attack on one would be regarded as an attack on the other. The only treaty she had signed was for a 30 year period with the Soviet Union providing for full scale mutual defence assistance. But because of the Sino-Soviet schism this treaty was soon forgotten and abrogated. This is the solitary example of China having entered into a treaty commitment. But China had been helping countries in Indo-China (Vietnam, Laos and Cambodia) militarily having no mutual defence pact with them. As such, it

was unlikely that China would have suddenly embraced Pakistan for such a pact, China had already been helping Pakistan with arms and this could have gone without a pact. China did not want anything more.[91]

Another object of Bhutto mission was said to be to persuade China to raise the Indo-Pak issue in the Security Council but it appeared that China did not like to start its UN career as Pakistan's champion as would have been the case if it had supported Pakistan if and when the latter raised allegations against India in the Security Council. China wanted to sponsor some important cause for which its reputation would have risen in the world community. Taking an egoistic view it could be said that China in the UN was more concerned with bigger world issues in its bid to make an initial impact and to direct fire on what it called 'US imperialists and Soviet revisionists' rather than be bogged down on secondary issues. Further, if China had agreed to sponsor the Pakistani case it would have found that the other four permanent members disassociated themselves from any impression of supporting the military suppression of the democratic movement in East Bengal.

The fact that the delegation was in China only for two days a major part of which they spent in exchanging courtesies and attending receptions shows that they had nothing business-like to discuss except that they were there on displaying its publicity aspect. No joint statement was issued at the end of the visit. The only important statement was the speech made by the acting foreign minister, Chi Peng-fei. In this speech, he said that 'the dispute between the two countries should be settled through consultations and not by resorting to force.' This was quite in conformity with what certain Anglo-American quarters had been insisting upon for some time. This also accepted the western version that the crisis in Bangladesh was a dispute between India and Pakistan. Chi Peng-fei, however, stressed that a reasonable settlement should be sought by the Pakistani people themselves to solve the East Bengal problem. This may be interpreted to mean a direct accord with the freedom fighters and that is what India had been advocating from the very beginning. But such a counsel was not likely to be relished in Pakistan.

China analysts felt that the statement of the acting Chinese

foreign minister, Chi, made at the banquet, was nothing more than a morale booster to Pakistan in the confrontation with India, whereas the main object of Bhutto mission was to extract a firm commitment from Peking to tie down Indian army divisions in both the sectors in the event of an Indo-Pakistani war. No promise of such action seemed to have been given. This shows that the Chinese were unwilling to commit themselves to anything that might risk the threat of Russian retaliation under the Indo-Soviet treaty.

According to some sinologists the possibility was that instead of being a party to the conflict, the Chinese would try to defuse the crisis before it reached the flash-point. In case the intractable Pak Generals did not pay heed to what the Chinese had told them and in a mood of desperation started war China would quietly tell them to stew in their own juice and face the consequences of their hard-headedness. This is what exactly happened after all. In the evening of 7 November Bhutto gave a return banquet at which Chou was present and made a brief speech. He did not speak a word about Indo-Pakistani relations. It was a mere courtesy speech in which he referred to 'the friendly relations and the cooperation between the two countries' and he requested Bhutto mission to convey the 'cordial regards and high considerations' of the Chinese government and people to Yahya Khan and the people of Pakistan.[92]

When on his return from Peking, Bhutto was asked if his mission had achieved any 'concrete results', he replied with a categorical 'yes'. He further spelt out the achievements of his mission when he declared: 'We are more than satisfied...we are now in full preparedness to maintain territorial integrity against foreign aggression.' Bhutto also said that if a war broke out between India and Pakistan the latter would have certain friends who would fight shoulder to shoulder with it without entering into a formal pact. He warned that any war between the two countries would be a total war and a house-to-house conflict, the waters of Ganga and Indus would be red as a result of bloodshed. The tone in which he made such statements may be said to have been born out of some sense of fulfilment of the objectives of his mission.

THE WAR AND CHINA

A Chinese delegation led by Li Shui-ching, a cabinet minister arrived in Pakistan in the third week of November to carry on negotiations about establishing a heavy engineering complex at Taxila. On 23 November in the presence of this delegation, Yahya Khan declared that within next ten days he would be found somewhere on the war front. It was almost a declaration of war and he was true to his word. Hardly had the Chinese delegation left Pakistan, did Yahya Khan declare war on India on Friday the 3 December 1971. The Soviet sources and for that matter Indian sources also felt that Pakistan would not have launched military operations against India on a particular day if it had not been fully assured of support by some outside power which in this case could not be any other than China. The significant point was that the ten days' notice expired exactly on the day when the Pakistani aircrafts started bombing Indian airports. Normally Peking takes its own time to make announcements regarding developments in which it is interested or involved but about the 'aggression' that India had committed on Pakistan on 3 December, *New China News Agency* made an announcement almost simultaneously with Pakistani radio barely half an hour after Pakistani aircrafts had attacked Indian airports. This clearly pointed to the collusion between Pakistan and China in their attempt to brand India as the aggressor.[93]

As a reaction to the recognition of Bangladesh government by India on 6 December, Peking Radio termed it as an Indian act of 'expansionism' and compared Bangladesh government with the Japanese puppet government in Manchuria which was recognised by the German and Italian fascist rulers alone. According to the Chinese publicity media, the Indian efforts had misfired as no other country had recognised it. This line of attack suggested that China would not think of recognising Bangladesh even after the war was over unless of course the internal situation there changed radically to Peking's liking.

The Chinese statements which were very bitter and scathing during the war period were significant from one point of view. Each Chinese statement which criticised India also included the Soviet Union; in fact every criticism of Indian policy was aimed

more at the Soviet policy because they felt that India itself could not take any step without the approval and support of the Soviet Union. So the main 'culprit' in the crisis was Russia at whose behest India was acting aggressively.[94] As regards the war, the Chinese openly argued that if the Soviet Union had not given military support to India, Mrs. Gandhi would not have adopted so belligerent a policy towards Pakistan. So Peking's real worry was Moscow's influence on New Delhi and that the core of its diplomatic objective was to try to check this influence. This also explains why Chinese support to Pakistan had been noticeably muted since the Indo-Soviet treaty was signed—an oblique admission of the effectiveness of Mrs. Gandhi's strategy.

However, though China could not take any effective step to help Pakistan it continued to indulge in name calling and what it could not do in deeds it sought to do through words. The Indian Charge d'Affaires walked out of a diplomatic reception on 9 December after the Chinese acting foreign minister Chi Peng-fei had attacked the Indian government. A few minutes later Chou En-lai walked over to the Pakistani ambassador and toasted Pakistani victory in the conflict with India. He assured Pakistani diplomat that 'the aggressors would soon be defeated'. The incident occurred at a reception held to mark Tanzania's national day. A similar walk out had taken place earlier on 29 November 1971 at the Albanian national day reception in Peking when the Soviet and Indian governments were attacked in the Albanian and Chinese speeches. The East European diplomats left first when the Albanian ambassador denounced what he called 'Soviet imperialism'. The Indian guests followed when the Chinese Vice-Premier Li Hsien-nien levelled charges against India in relation to Pakistan and East Bengal.

China did try to help Pakistan in its own way during the war period but it did not succeed. Two incidents corroborate this assumption. When the war was through for about a week China tried to create some trouble for India. On 10 December the Prime Minister of India was informed of Chinese troops movements on Indo-Tibetan border. On 11 December Mrs. Gandhi sent D.P. Dhar post haste to Moscow and the same day she spoke at a students' meeting in Delhi about grave dangers to Indian security. On 12 December Soviet troops started making movements on Sino-Soviet border. The Chinese immediately ordered their forces to stay back

and keep to their original positions on Sino-Indian border. In this connection it should also be stressed that India was not off the guard with regard to security threats from the Chinese side. After the end of the monsoon and before the advent of winter, India started sending forces in South Sikkim as part of preparations to resist any possible Chinese counter pressure designed to relieve Pakistani forces in East Bengal in the event of an armed conflict. India took this precautionary step even though there was no indication then that the Chinese were moving troops in Tibet or Sinkiang.

Another incident was reported to be associated with the Chinese proposed move to evacuate Pakistani troops from East Pakistan by ships under the Chinese flag. Now the problem was what the Chinese would do if these ships were attacked by Indian forces which was a certainty as the Indian troops had already blocked both the sea ports of East Bengal. The Chinese were afraid of the Soviet reactions which such a step on their part would evoke. In brief, first India and then Soviet Union would not allow any Chinese armed intervention to go unchallenged. On this understanding China refrained from making a move which would have brought it in direct conflict with India and the Soviet Union.

Some observers of the Chinese affairs detected in the Chinese behaviour a tactics of double dealing designed to convince Pakistan that China wanted to help its ally but it could not for very weighty considerations. The stark fact was that China was not prepared to run any risk to get actively involved in the Indo-Pakistani conflict. The reported contingency plans for helping to evacuate defeated Pakistani troops were regarded as a face-saving alternative to the loss of prestige involved in standing aside. Secondly, the Chinese realised that if they had dared to frustrate Indian success, the war would have spread involving other nations also. This the Chinese wanted to avoid.

Having found itself in such a situation of helplessness, China asked America to make a military move to save the situation for Pakistan and prevent the Bangladesh forces and Indian army from presenting the world with a *fait accompli.* Russian intelligence sources discovered that President Nixon had decided to make a show of strength as a last ditch effort to enforce a ceasefire before

Pakistan was completely routed from Bangladesh soil. This took the form of sending the seventh fleet to Bay of Bengal. The Indian army was already warned and the Russian navy came to our help. This common strategy foiled the American plan initiated at the instance of the Chinese.

AFTER THE LIBERATION

After the surrender of Pakistani troops, the Chinese government issued on 16 December a statement violently attacking Indian and Soviet governments. It particularly accused Indian forces of committing 'most brutal atrocities' and Indian government of 'wild ambitions of expansionism'. India was also blamed for trying to destroy the whole of Pakistan in the wake of which other neighbouring countries would also be endangered. Recalling the days of Sino-Indian conflict of 1962 China described Mrs. Gandhi's policy as a projection of 'Nehru's philosophy' which later proved to be a dream. The Soviet Union was criticised for trying 'to strengthen its control over India and thereby to proceed to contend with the other super powers for hegemony in the whole of the south Asian subcontinent and the Indian Ocean. It was further castigated for attempting to turn India into a sub-super power on the south Asian sub-continent as its assistant and partner in committing aggression against Asian countries.[95]

Again on 26 December speaking in Peking in honour of a visiting Iraqi government delegation, the Chinese Deputy Premier Li Hsien-nien drew a parallel between the Indo-Pak conflict and the Palestinian question which, in his opinion, had both common and complementary characters. China considered the Indo-Pak conflict and the Palestinian question as the two main issues of a political offensive that coincided with Peking's entry into the UN. It is worth noting that all these remarks were aimed at the entire Muslim world with which India's relations were cordial and where the Soviet stock was also very high. What Peking wanted was to create bad blood between India and the Soviet Union on one hand and the Arab people on the other.

Another step that Peking took out of frustration was to lodge a protest with New Delhi on 18 December against incursions into Tibet. The Chinese note said that even Indian soldiers had crossed

into China's Tibetan province from the 'Indian protectorate' of Sikkim on 10 December for reconnaissance purposes and demanded that India should immediately stop its 'incursions'. The Indian reply called the Chinese charges 'totally without foundation' and as such ignored it. Another protest followed on 27 December charging that eight Indian soldiers and an Indian aircraft encroached Chinese territory from Sikkim on 15 December.[96] The Indian government again took no serious notice of this protest and rejected it with a routine denial.

But why these pinpricks? It was a crude effort on the part of China to see that India remained pre-occupied with defence worries. The Chinese probably felt that by such petty harassment on Himalayan frontier India would be prevented from deriving full advantage of strategy and prestige from the military victory over Pakistan. Since Indian frontiers with China were well guarded Indian government was least worried by the Chinese manoeuvrings. But there was some mystery that both alleged incursions took place on Sikkim border and in 1965 also it was on Sikkim border that similar charges were levelled. It is because Peking had an eye on weaning Sikkim away from the Indian orbit. With the Chinese influence already high in Nepal, Peking wanted to strengthen its position in the Himalayan states as compensation for its loss of influence in Bangladesh.[97]

Another motive of all these accusations could be to console Pakistan that China had not reconciled to the loss of Bangladesh and that it would continue to do something or the other to help Pakistan. At best it could be seen as a futile demonstration of China's oft-proclaimed solidarity with Pakistan that the defeat of Pakistan in the war was their own and the victory of India as threat of Russia. The Chinese attempt to brow beat India appeared to be a manifestation of guilt-consciousness or antics of a bully. After the end of war, in favour of Bangladesh, China felt sorry for not being able to influence the course of events in its neighbourhood and to help a 'valued friend', something which no super power could allow to happen. Moreover, since 1962 China had developed the psychology of a bully which made it say that no diplomatic or territorial changes should take place without its acquiescence in South and South-east Asia where China felt its supremacy was paramount. But the result of this war irreparably hurt the vanity of China.

Till the year end the Chinese did not seem to have reconciled with the situation that had arisen in the wake of emergence of Bangladesh as an independent state. On 23 December the official news agency *Hsinhua* repeated the old allegation that 'India's invasion' of Pakistan was part of a 'long premeditated dirty deal' between the Soviet Union and India. It said: 'Soviet revisionist social imperialism was pursuing frenziedly its policy of setting Asians against Asians to realise its 'vicious aim' to control South Asia sub-continent and the Indian Ocean. Making use of the expansionist ambitions for a greater Indian empire, the Soviets instigated the Indian reactionaries to set themselves against other Asian countries and create tension incessantly. At the close of the year, in a review of the events during 1971 and forecast for 1972, a commentary issued by the Chinese news agency said that Russia would be further 'isolated' and 'punishment' would be given to India for her role in the Indo-Pakistan war.

12

SUMMARY AND CONCLUSIONS

In his first broadcast after assuming reins of the interim government on 2 September 1946, Nehru referred to China as a neighbouring country with a mighty past. The conspicuous characteristic of the past era was marked by an abiding friendship between the two countries. He hoped China would overcome all the domestic troubles and may play a big role in furthering world peace. In expressing these sentiments he was reflecting the true feelings of the Indian people for the Chinese people.

On 30 December 1949, the government of India accorded recognition to the new government headed by Mao Tse-tung and Chou En-lai as Prime Minister. The recognition was delayed by a few days in deference to the wishes of the UK government which was also interested in being the first few states to extend recognition to new Chinese government. In justifying the government decision, Nehru said it was not a question of approving or disapproving a new regime; it was the question of recognising the major event of history and of dealing with it.

The Chinese response was not a dignified one. The key note was struck when the Chinese leaders branded Nehru 'a running dog of imperialism'. A Chinese comment lumped Nehru with Bao Dai, Syngman Rhee and Chiang Kai-shek as among 'the dregs of

mankind'. Mao was reported to have cabled to the communist party chief in India on 19 October 1949 that the communist party of India with the unity and struggle of all Indian patriots would not allow India to remain under the yoke of imperialism and like China would emerge as the socialist peoples' democracy in India.[98]

Even on the Korean issue in which India did so much for China, Peking's response was devoid of decency and towards India's efforts to mediate on the prisoners of war issue scornful. Krishna Menon's compromise formula was described by the Chinese spokesmen as an illegal resolution which had as its basic content the United States' principle of voluntary repatriation under an Indian cloak'.[99] Only after the Korean truce talks began did Peking's policies begin to shift towards a more conciliatory line. But this was in keeping with a general shift in international communist tactics.

India, on its part, tried to keep China befriended by all means at its disposal, the conspicuous being its consistently sponsoring China's case for recognition and its right to occupy the Chinese seat in the UN. Besides, India voted against a UN resolution branding China aggressor in Korea, criticised US actions to neutralise Taiwan in 1950 and declined to attend the conference convened in San Francisco in 1951 to sign a peace treaty with Japan as, among other reasons, China was not a party to it. In 1951 India introduced a resolution in the General Assembly on prisoners of war in Korea and Nehru declared that the resolution was intended to accommodate Chinese view on that question.

A major event in Sino-Indian relations took place on 29 April 1954 when the two countries signed an agreement on trade and intercourse between India and Tibet. India was helpless in continuing to consider Tibet an absolutely independent state. India formally abandoned its traditional position that Tibet should be an autonomous buffer zone. Besides, India gave up all extra territorial rights and privileges in Tibet inherited from the British days. The agreement specified trade agencies, markets and pilgrim routes. The Kashgar consulate was not allowed to function as Sinkiang was declared a closed zone. In the preamble to this agreement, the five principles of peaceful coexistence, the Panchsheel, were mentioned.

The Chinese seemed to have timed the signing of the accord with the Colombo conference in Ceylon (Sri Lanka), as Chinese thereby wanted to score the point of being reasonable and peaceful towards an Asian power. It was also linked with the opening of the Geneva conference on Indo-China. This conference began at a moment when China could benefit from Indian goodwill and the europhic atmosphere created by the accord.

In defending the accord, Nehru observed 'we have done nothing better in the field of foreign affairs during the last six years than signing the agreement on Tibet. The agreement is good not only for our country but also for the rest of the world.' The socalled Hindi-Chini bhai bhai era had begun and there was a galore of good will missions exchanged between the two countries. But this illusory era was not to last long and all that followed gave us a rude shock that we were gradually drifting into the world of make-believe. In this context, Mrs. Laxmi Menon, deputy minister of foreign affairs, said that the signing of the Sino-Indian agreement was a signal for the start of our trouble on our northern frontiers.

At dawn on 20 October 1962 twenty thousand Chinese troops attacked NEFA, the eastern border with China. It was a full scale and well planned attack launched skilfully across the high mountain range which marked the boundaries between the two countries. The Chinese army also attacked Ladakh at the north west end of the frontier where the Aksai Chin road was a bone of contention. The Chinese attack was very fast and severe so much so that within a few hours they drove to within seven miles into the Indian territory. On the second day, China opened a third front near the Burma border. Within four days they occupied all the land which they claimed to be theirs.

On 24 October, the Chinese offered that both sides withdraw 20 km from the current line of actual control. As the line of actual control had been pushed deep into Indian territory by four days of steady Chinese advance, the terms were too humiliating to be acceptable to India. India suggested that negotiations could be held only if the Chinese had withdrawn to positions held before 8 September 1962.

On 26 October Nehru wrote to most of the heads of government

explaining Indian position in the dispute and asked for their moral support. The government also wrote to the Indian missions to plead Indian case throughout Asia and Africa. The most encouraging response was from the West; US, UK and Canada particularly offered not only sympathy but also material help. The US responded immediately with most of the material required by the Indian army. China warned twenty Afro-Asian heads of state that US and India would enlarge the area of conflict.

On 8 November, China offered its second ceasefire plan which repeated the earlier terms, the main of which was that both sides withdraw their troops 20 km behind the lines held on 7 November 1959. India rejected it on the ground that it would leave China in possession of 15,000 sq. miles of territory which belonged to India. China resumed fighting on 15 November capturing more area including the one which was in the neighbourhood of oil fields in Assam.

In a dramatic move, the Chinese on 21 November announced unilateral ceasefire along the entire Indian border and promised to begin pulling back troops on 1 December 1962. This was mere repetition of what the Chinese had offered two weeks back. The Chinese forces would withdraw 20 km behind the line of actual control of 7 November 1959. This would mean that the Chinese would retain control of the Aksai Chin road and the area west of it that they had occupied. In the northeast, China would respect the Mc Mahon line.

Significantly enough, China's announcement was made when Kennedy in response to Khrushchev's assurance that all Soviet offensive missiles in Cuba would be withdrawn within twenty days had lifted the naval blockade. Now both US and Soviet Union were in a position to look up to China if the latter continued to go on with its war on India.

Representatives of six nonaligned countries, Ceylon, Burma, Cambodia, Ghana, Indonesia and the United Arab Republic met in Colombo from 10 to 12 December 1962 to discuss the Sino-Indian dispute. The proceedings were held in camera. The spokesman of the conference said that the conference was seeking mediation to enable the two sides to resume negotiations and the conference

would itself pass no judgement on merits of the case of each side as it was conscious of its limitations. The communique issued on 12 December 1962 merely said that the unanimous agreement had been reached and its contents would be revealed only when the two sides gave their reactions.

The contents of the communique were published on 10 January 1963 after they had been conveyed to both the countries. What they proposed, after clarification, was that in the west, the Chinese should withdraw 20 km from the line of actual control as it existed on 8 September 1962, that is the date on which the Chinese had started entering surreptitiously into the Indian region. It meant that India wanted to get back to the 43 army posts which it had set up there and which later were occupied by the Chinese. India was prepared to accept the location, number and composition of the Chinese posts as they were before the conflict began. China categorically said that the Indian posts occupied by the Chinese would remain in its hands.

Sino-Indian tensions involved more than a psychological problem. They had never been rooted in the controversy over a few uninhabited border areas. If China had desired a border settlement one could easily have been achieved in the mid-fifties. But Peking deliberately kept the matter open while the situation was gradually becoming more complicated as a result of the rebellion in Tibet, the deterioration in Sino-Soviet relations and the increasing feeling in China that India stood in the way of her overall regional ambitions. So China opted for a military solution. Liu Shao-chi aggressively said during the aggression period that India had to be hit on the head again and again and again.[100]

There seemed to be no chance of Sino-Indian relations being improved until an agreement was reached on the territory that China had occupied. It was the height of absurdity to assume that China would repent its aggression as a result of which it had captured a lot of Indian territory. The fact of the matter was that ever since then China's hostility towards India had grown as reflected in its support to Pakistan in developing the latter's animosity towards India, efforts to work against Indian interests in Nepal and Bhutan, its refusal to recognise Sikkim as part of India and support to subversion in the North Eastern Frontier

Agency. In brief, China had worked against India everywhere. Even assuming for the sake of one's satisfaction that border agreement was sealed, Chinese friendship could not be taken for granted because Peking's ambitions for Asian leadership would remain unchanged and India as rival would remain a hindrance.

The Chinese foreign minister Chen Yi was in Pakistan in the last week of August 1965. During his talks with Pak leaders he assured them of his government's support to Pakistan to repel armed Indian aggression wheresoever it occurred. China tried to play its second card on 7 September when the war broke out between India and Pakistan. Peking described it as naked aggression by India and as it was committed against a neighbouring country it should be a matter of concern to all the Asian nations. China also warned India against a chain of consequences which would follow.

Next day, 8 September, China accused India of 'military aggression and provocation' along the Sino-Indian border. Pak ambassador in Peking called on Chinese president Liu Shao chi to suggest what action China should take against India. Probably as a result of this meeting China delivered a formal note to India demanding withdrawal of Indian troops from the contested posts on the Sikkim border. India was also accused of violating China's border in conjunction with aggression against Pakistan.

It was often questioned, why did China choose Sikkim where the border was not in dispute? It was a pressure tactics on the part of China to brow beat India in the hope of gaining goodwill of Pakistan. It was also an attempt on the part of the Chinese to question India's historic rights to speak for Sikkim. It was a far-fetched assumption that Chinese forces, in case the conflict prolonged, would join hands with Pak forces in East Pakistan and cut off Assam or NEFA from India. But this may have been one of the objectives of China.

This sort of pinpricks went on intermittently during the war. On 16 September, Peking served an ultimatum to India demanding that certain border posts be dismantled within 72 hours failing which India would face the 'penalty of grave consequences'. Shastri announced in the Parliament that the Chinese could dismantle the

posts if there were any on the Chinese side of the border. India also proposed a joint inspection of the region concerned. On 22 September Chinese announced that India had complied with their demands. India did nothing of the sort; the Chinese themselves may have done that if at all they had to do that. After a strong pressure from America and the USSR, Pakistan agreed to ceasefire to end war. The main reason that led Pakistan to take this step was the inadequacy of ammunition stocks and spare parts of American arms. The Indian army had caused heavy damage to the weaponry supplied by America.

China's attitude towards Bangladesh crisis was an aspect of China's total policy towards Indian sub-continent. Let us have a brief review of it. Ever since its inception in 1949, the communist China had striven to keep cordial relations with both the countries – India and Pakistan. It has been easy for China to keep Pakistan humoured because it could never dream of being a rival to it in acquiring political influence in the sub-continent. But India has always been regarded a serious contender to China's ambitions in Asia. Pakistan could thus be helpful to China in realising its political aims because it could not have any ambitions which might clash with those of China whereas with India they came in direct clash. So Sino-Pak relations made any sense only in the context of China's given bid for influence in Asia against the feared encroachment of Russian and Indian influence.[101]

Even when Pakistan joined the SEATO in 1954, ostensibly to help America to 'contain and counter Chinese communist expansion', the Chinese did not feel much concerned though they let loose a verbal skirmish. They thought that this move on the part of Pakistan was aimed at augmenting its military strength vis-a-vis India. And India, the more powerful of the two, was with China, having earlier signed the Panchsheel agreement on 29 April 1954. The Chinese further believed that the main cause of tension between India and Pakistan was the Kashmir issue on which it had already decided to adopt an impartial attitude. The Chinese thinking, therefore, was that if on Indo-Pak issues China remained neutral, whatever anti-Chinese element was there in Pakistan politics would soon disappear.[102] It is why in 1957 when the Indian people were swearing by the slogan, 'Hindi-Chini bhai bhai', the Chinese declared that they had taken an attitude of 'non-involvement' on the Kashmir issue.

In 1959 Tibetan uprising took place and Dalai Lama had to leave for India. All this upset the Chinese who thought that India was implicated in the trouble in Tibet. In May 1961, U2 incident took place in which Pakistan gave all facilities to the American pilots to start their spying flights from Peshawar airport. Russia was enraged at the Pakistani collaboration with America in launching its espionage flights from the Pakistani territory. The fact that in early sixties India and the Soviet Union had developed hostile relations with China gave a chance to Islamabad to come closer to Peking.

On May 3, 1962 China and Pakistan simultaneously announced their desire to demarcate the boundaries between them and almost within a year a boundary agreement was signed on 2 March 1963 by which Pakistan ceded to China nearly 2050 sq. miles of Kashmir territory which was so far under its occupation. In view of these territorial concessions which were of great strategic value, there was a sudden change in the Chinese policy of 'non-involvement' in the Kashmir issue and it became one of open support to the Kashmiri people's struggle to resist Indian 'tyrannical' rule. Relations with India were getting worse every day which culminated in the Chinese aggression on India in October 1962. Thereafter, there appeared to be no possibility of an early normalisation of relations between these two Asian countries. During the 1965 Indo-Pak conflict there came about a strong collusion between Pakistan and China because both wanted to settle old scores with India. On 5 September 1965 when Pakistan launched its formidable offensive to capture Kashmir, Peking was first silent but when it found that the tide was turning against Pakistan it threatened India with dire consequences if the 'aggression' continued. A more serious allegation was that India had constructed bunkers along the Sikkim border on Chinese soil. However, both protests were turned down by India.

Of all the countries, China was the only one to feel unhappy with the Tashkent agreement signed in January 1966 between India and Pakistan at the initiative of the Soviet Union. The Chinese probably wanted the hostilities to continue in the hope that they would weaken India economically as well as militarily. Another phase in Sino-Pakistani relations began with the Chinese arms aid going to Pakistan and this coincided with Yahya Khan's visit to Peking in November 1970. The Chinese were reported to have

armed three mountain divisions of the Pakistan army besides supplying them tanks and MiGs and training their officers in guerrilla warfare. Since the Chinese alone could not meet all the requirements of Pakistan they allowed it to go close to the West to get more arms aid which would automatically mean less aid to India. Now the Chinese aim was to see that a counter-weight to India, Pakistan, became militarily strong.

As a result of the successful end of the war in Bangladesh, China's two basic assumptions regarding the sub-continent had collapsed. First, China had all along taken it for granted that Pakistan could be used to offset New Delhi's influence in the region. This assumption became invalid in view of the disintegration of Pakistan which was after the war much reduced in size, population and resources and strategically became more vulnerable to Indian attacks. Secondly, China had been so used to India's policy of low posture, a policy of non-retaliation and accommodation that in all probability it did not occur to it that India would go so far as to sign a defence treaty with the Soviet Union and, finally, with its help and sanction, would launch a massive attack to liberate Bangladesh. No Chinese leaders could ever believe that India would be so daring and phenomenally brave as to fight a war on behalf of another nation, against heavy odds. So far India talked of principles, this time it showed in action that no price was too high for India to pay in upholding certain ideals. The Chinese did not believe it so far.

Actually, the emergence of Bangladesh as a sovereign independent nation should in no way have affected China's legitimate interests but in the calculation of Peking's policy-makers it was more important to keep Pakistan intact as a two-winged countercheck to the growing Indian power than the success of a people's liberation struggle. In fact, the thought that the emergence of Bangladesh might bring about a major change in the regional balance was unwelcome not only in Peking but in several other capitals in Asia as well as in Europe. However, if Chinese interests lay in maintaining Pakistan as a strong rival to a hostile India, it could serve that purpose only so long as Pakistan remained strong and united. A Pakistan undermined by the necessity of waging a protracted and expensive campaign of military repression in Bangladesh could not be much of a challenge to India in any way.

The Chinese might have said anything to console Pakistanis but in heart of their hearts, they were conscious that after Bangladesh liberation Pakistan could not continue to be that Pakistan on which it had started leaning for exerting pressure on India some ten years ago.

As a result of the establishment of Bangladesh, China faced some awkward consequences. First, China was no more the sole focus of attention of the third world; India emerged as a rival force presenting a more attractive alternative model to be followed in national and international spheres. Secondly, on ideological front it had turned out to be a Chinese defeat at the hands of Russia. So far both Russia and China were vying with each other in claiming to be the true leader of liberation movements in Asia and Africa. But in this case Russia established its revolutionary credentials much better than China as it was with Russia's assurance of support that Bangladesh could achieve its independence. Maoists may pose themselves as champions of the colonial victims but they do not hesitate to betray the movement if they find that their national interest calls for a deal with reactionary elements. This is what they had done during Bangladesh crisis. What they were more interested in was to find a chance to malign the Soviet Union. Thirdly, one of the main aims of Chinese foreign policy has been to keep India engaged by the Pakistani threat and specially after the Indo-Soviet treaty it became a diplomatic imperative. As a result of war, with Pakistan cut to size, despite all foreign assistance, that situation was completely changed. On the other hand, India added to its military strength by getting an ally of 7.5 crore people. China's options were closed on this front; it was neutralised.

REFERENCES

1. Timothy George *et al. Security in Southern Asia : India and the Great Powers*, p. 47.

2. John Rowland : *A History of Sino-Indian Relations, Hostile Co-existence*, p. 174.

3. Timothy George *et, al., op. cit.*, pp. 30-31.

4. See Lt. Gen. B.M. Kaul, *Confrontation with Pakistan*, p. 185.

5. John Rowland *op. cit.*, p. 180.

6. A.G. Noornani, *Our Credibility and Negligence*, p. 12.

7. Gregory Clark, *In Fear of China*, p. 58.

8. John Rowland, *op. cit.*, p. 169.

9. *Ibid.*, p. 85.

10. *Ibid.*, p. 208.

11. See *Peking Review* No. 46, 12 November 1971, pp. 5 and 23.

12. For American comments see editorials in *New York Times* and *Washington Post* dated 10 August 1971 and *Christian Sciences Monitor* 11 August 1971.

13. Aamlendu Das Gupta, 'China on Bangladesh' in the *Statesman*, 6 December 1971.

14. See Richard Harris 'China's Attitude to the Indo-Pak Conflict' in *The Times* (London) 13 December 1971.

15. JNU Seminar, *Search for a China Policy*, 21-22 January 1989, p. 5.

16. K.M. Panikkar, *In Two Chinas*, p. 44.

17. Dorothy Woodman, *Himalayan Frontier*, pp. 216-17.

18. John Rowland, *op., cit.*, p. 82.

19. See for details, P.C. Chakravarty, *India-China Relations*. As far back as 1940 Mao referred to the two camps in which the third world had no peace. See. A. Appadorai in *International Studies*. July-Oct. 1963, p. 16.

20. S.S. Khera, *India's Defence Problem*, p. 137.

21. N. Maxwell, *India's China War*, p. 261.

22. *Ibid.*

23. A.D. Gorwala, *Danger from Communist China*, p. 40.

24. Parushottam L. Mehra, *Negotiating with the Chinese 1846-1987*, p. 102, cites Rushbrook Williams, The *State of Pakistan*, p. 120.

25. A. Appadorai, 'Chinese aggression and India', *International Studies*, July-October 1963, p. 405.

26. *Ibid.*

27. Amyia Rao and B.G. Rao, *Six Thousand Days*, p. 99.

28. *Ibid.*

29. Dorothy Woodman, *op. cit.*, p. 210.

30. K.M. Panikkar, *op. cit.*, p. 105.

31. For details, See J. Rowland *op. cit.*, pp. 56, 66-68.

32. Karunakar Gupta, *The Hidden History of Sino-Indian Frontier*, pp. 54-55.

33. B.N. Mullik, *Chinese Betrayal*, p. 147.

34. *Hindu*, 18 November 1950, quoted in A. Roy and B.G. Roy, *op. cit.*

35. Rajya Sabha Debate, 10 October 1950, cited in A Roy and B.G. Roy, *op. cit.*, p. 89.

36. Parushottam L. Mehra, India China and Tibet in V. Grover, volume 3, p. 477.

37. J. Rowland, *op. cit.*, p. 84.

38. *Eastern Economists*, 7 May 1954, p. 741.

39. S.C. Bhatt, *The Triangle, India, Nepal and China: A Study of Treaty Relations*, p. 207, R.K. Jain quoted.

40. A.D. Gorwale, *op. cit.*, p. 41. For similar subjects see B.N. Mullik, pp. 152-56.

41. B.N. Mullik, *op. cit.*, pp. 216-17.

42. D.R. Mankekar, *The Guilty Men of 1962*, p. 30.

43. S.C. Bhatt, *op. cit.*, p. 207.

44. External Affairs Ministry, *India-China Border Dispute*, p. 10.

45. See, *Times of India*, 11 October 1954, editorial comment.

46. B.N. Mullik, *My Years with Nehru*, 1948-64, p. 215.

47. *Peking Review*, 3 May 1961 quoted in Maxwell. *op. cit.*

48. T.S. Murthi, *Pattern of Peace*, pp. 122.

49. A. Roy and B.G. Roy, *op. cit.*, p. 133.

50. S.C. Bhatt, *op. cit.*, p. 207.

51. S.S. Khera, *India's Defence Probelm*, pp. 135-36.

52. Brig. J. Dalvi, *Himalayan Blunder*, p. 365.

53. *Ibid.*, p. 371.

54. D.R. Mankekar, *op. cit.*, p. 89.

55. Sudhir Ghosh, *Gandhi's Emissary*, p. 329.

56. N. Maxwell, *op. cit.*, p. 425.

57. Brig. J. Dalvi ,*op. cit.*, pp. 479-80.

58. Dorothy Woodman, *op. cit.*, p. 293.

59. Brig. J. Dalvi, *op. cit.*, p. 405.

60. Dorothy Woodman, *op. cit.*, p. 214.

61. N. Maxwell, *op. cit.*, p. 378.

62. S.S. Khera, *op. cit.*, p. 138.

63. N. Maxwell, *op. cit.*, p. 349.

64. *Lok Sabha Debates* 10 December 1962, vol. XI, col. 5088-92 vide *White Paper*, vol. VIII, p. 35-38.

65. N. Maxwell, *op. cit.*, p. 431.

66. Nehru's letter to Chou-En-lai, 1 May 1963. *White Paper*, vol. IX

67. Chou's letter to Nehru, 20 April 1963, *White Paper*, vol. IX, p. 13.

68. *Lok Sabha Debates*, in *White Paper*, vol. VIII, *op. cit.*, n. 43.

69. Chinese Memorandum 29 December 1962. *White Paper*, vol. VIII, pp. 39-46.

70. Government of India, Publication—*China Discards Colombo Proposals*, p. 17.

71. *Chinese Press Release* 3005 dated 15 February 1963.

72. See *White Paper*, vol. X, p. 306 and also Maxwell, *op. cit.*, p. 432.

73. N. Maxwell, *op. cit.*, p. 419.

74. Hodson H.V. *The Great Divide*,'p. 431.

75. Sudhir Ghosh, *op. cit.*, p. 306.

76. J. Dalvi, *op. cit.*, p. 74

77. Yertz Burgar, Ohlson and Brozski, cited by Harish Kapur, *India's Foreign Policy, Shadows and Substance*, p. 112.

78. *Ibid.*, p. 113.

79. See *Hindu*, 8 October 1964.

80. See Harish Kapur *op. cit.*

81. Agency news flashed in all national dailies vide *Hindu* and *Statesman*, 26 September. 1965.

82. Russel Brines, *Indo-Pak Conflict*, p. 254.

83. *New York Times*, 9 September 1965 cited in Russel Brines, p. 326.

84. Pran Chopra, *Uncertain India*, p. 316.

85. John Rowland, *op. cit.*, p. 208.

86. For an analysis of China's stand on Bangladesh crisis, see Richard Hariss, China's attitude to the Indo-Pak conflict, also *Times of India*, 13 December and 29 March 1971.

87. *Tribune* (Ambala), 18 March 1971.

88. *Statesman*, 8 April 1971 also *International Herald, Tribune*, 8 April 1971.

89. *Times of India*, 13 April 1971.

90. *Guardian* (Manchester), 18 June 1971 from John Giffings for an analysis of China's motives.

91. See *Indian Express*, 13 December 1971 from B.K. Tiwari in Hongkong.

92. See *Free Press Journal*, 9 April 1971, and *National Herald*, 23 March 1979 for editorial comments.

93. *Hindu*, 8 December 1971 edit: 'China's guilty conscience'.

94. S.K. Ghosh 'The Indo-Soviet Treaty and China' in V. Grover, vol. 3, p. 517.

95. For details, see *Hindustan Standard* (Calcutta), 10 November 1977 also *News Review on China* (IDSA), November 1971, p. 43.

96. *Statesman,* 30 March 1971, also *News Review on China* (IDSA), November 1971, p. 45.

97. *Peking Review* No. 46, 12 November 1971, pp. 5 and 23.

98. *The Communist,* Bombay cited in John Rowland *op.cit.* p. 82.

99. *Ibid.*

100. Council on Foreign Relations, *India and the United States,* p. 47.

101. *Times of India,* 29 March 1971 from G.M. Telang in Hongkong.

102. *Hindustan Times,* 25 November 1971, from T.J.S. George in Hongkong.

INDEX

AF553405